Contents

On The Cover:
The John Gerraghty Convertible as photographed by Ralph Poole. Courtesy the Batchelor Archives / Ron Kellog Collection. A telephone call from Thom Taylor reminded us that this and all the Archives could be accessed through Ron Kellog. We talked, selected, paid and now it's yours!

HOP UP CONTRIBUTORS

MARK MORTON — Publisher/Editor   DREW HARDIN — Managing Editor

DOUG ANDERSON, PETER T. BENNETT, BURNS BERRYMAN, JIM CHINI, DOUG CLARK, CHARLIE CRUZ, ALBERT DRAKE, JOE EDDY, DAIN GINGERELLI, JON GOBETTI, KEN GROSS, KERRY HORAN, TONY HUNTIMER, AARON KAHAN, RON KELLOGG, DON MONTGOMERY, MARK MORTON, SHERM PORTER, CHUCK SARNO, TOM SEWELL, COCO SHINOMIYA, DAVE SIMARD, DAVID SIMON, THOM TAYLOR, TONY THACKER, RON THUMS PETER VINCENT, KEITH WEESNER

COCO SHINOMIYA/MONSTER X @ HEY POSER INDUSTRIES — Art Direction

Indicia

Hop Up Volume 2 is published by **Hop Up Products**, LLC, dba Hop Up Magazine, P.O. Box 790, Riverside, CA 92502.

Printed in the USA, of course. ISBN 0-9675570-1-1

PHOTO: PETER VINCENT

Mort's Shorts

The Golden Anniversary. Fifty years of *Hop Up*. Well, not quite. It was AWAY for most of those years. In this Annual, Volume II, we celebrate 50 years of Hop Up Style in the building, fixing, using and iconization of traditional rods and customs.

During most of that half-century there were a few Rodneys doing traditional cars; they were cats who didn't much care that fashion was escaping them. They didn't mind that their cars weren't making the covers of the big magazines and that they were not being credited with setting trends. They WERE living the life of hot rod types who used their cars in a type of "Civil War Reenactment" of how it had been done in another time. There was no romance for a "simpler" time; there wasn't any of the nostalgia for poodle skirts and fuzzy dice, or "Ban the Bomb," or Eisenhower or any of the rest. The guys just thought that a relatively un-evolved hot rod was a satisfying way to get their yuks in a world that didn't much care. Individualists.

Their forebears had been individualistic because they were experimenting with a modern, evolving, "keep up with fashion and performance" art form. Traditional rodders between 1960-1990 were individualistic because they did NOT want to keep up, did

NOT want to evolve, and did NOT curry the attention of the masses, or the favor of the magazines. This population has grown, albeit not in any great numbers that have modified the thinking of the big publishing companies. There have been new arrivals in the hobby who have chosen traditional bents, there have been a few "converts" (some of whose motives are suspect), and there is the Great Greasy Hope.

Not that real Hop Up types care if the thing is perpetuated for all time. But if we see that some group endorses the base style, the guttural vibration that radiates from Hop Up Iron, then they're welcomed and embraced. If some of them are a bit more interested in fame, attention, credit and all, well, that's probably OK too. And if the cars are only a fashion accessory, a bauble that is part of the outfit—another charm on the bracelet—well, we have always had less-than-sincere aficionados around. You seek your own level. To our relief, the majority of the younger traditionalists are imprinted with truth.

en hop up veritas.

And those tail-draggin' customs? They just about crapped out in the past 50 years, but a few individuals missed them and saw to it that there were venues and groups and publications available and VIOLA! We see as much growth in the traditional custom category as we do rods. Some people who would never "get" hot rods, might just "get" customs. *Hop Up* was the original source of rod and custom cars presented together; and we got customs here, too, as is fitting.

So *Hop Up*, in this second Annual, continues to have its greasy thumb on the pulse of that hot rod and custom truth. And while the entire staff at Hop Up World Headquarters (right here in River City) is dedicated to the continued presentation of that truth, we know, too, that our continued success will inevitably lead us to a crossroads. Growth and opportunity always lead one to a decision-making moment where the fiscal intersects with the visceral and one has to make a choice. We know why *Hop Up* is so well received and, in case you're wondering, the choice has already been made.

That's why we're all here.

Hop Up Honor. Stay Honor.

Rods & Customs

River City Rod 'n' Custom Roundup—podnuh!

Hop Up 2001 feature cars are grouped here for your approval. And you'll approve, boys. You will approve. Turn the page. Take it in. Note that car owners who "get it" often select *Hop Up* as the first-ever to publish feature articles about their standout cars. They reckon that the tone, the attitude, the visceral, the truth evoked from a book will define whether their double-throw-down, cool-ass rides should appear there. Or not. You got a good one for *Hop Up 2002*, Volume III?

Betcha do.

PHOTO: DEAN BATCHELOR/COURTESY THE RON KELLOG COLLECTION

BRENT BELL'S '32 FORD 5-WINDOW COUPE

BRENT HAD PLANNED TO BUILD A BEATER. He already had a greaser roadster and a greaser Merc, and he just wanted a closed hot rod to throw in the mix to shelter his family a little better when the weather was inclement.

He already had most of the parts it was gonna take and had literally completed the rolling chassis with small-block Chevy, Muncie four-speed, 9-inch Ford rear gears…and the body still had not appeared. One day Brent's Ol' Man says, "Hey, you know, a friend of mine is going another way with his Deuce project and has decided to sell his 5-window body. Interested?" He was, they did, and the thrash was on.

This is no hill, they thought. The body already had primer on it, even included an old-timey tuck-and-rolled seat, so they commenced to bolt it on the chassis. Then Brent thought, "Well, let's scuff it up and get some DP90 on it." And then they blocked it out a little. Then some more. The next coat of primer came out of the gun real smooth. They looked at one another and concurrently said, "Let's get Lou!!!"

Lou (Dreamer's Creations in Downey, California) is their paint guy. They had decided to go black and…they never went back. Once Lou-Lou got involved, this thing was going to be a diamond. (So much for the beater theory.) But that seems to be the way with most of these projects: When you are putting your own hands on them, the next degree of effort is easy to contribute. And the next. And the next.

This is a nice car, boys. Good call.

There is more to the aesthetic than just paint. Brent had a vision of the way his car should sit, sound and drive, too. He's the son of a motorcycle/hot rod type (Hop Up Guy) and got the fever pretty early on. He's

Above: Black-on-black car kind of "lays down." You end up walking close to it, finding much to appreciate. **From left to right:** "Stealth" look works good on the Deuce 5-window; we see the whole car, as opposed to just a set of wheels, or paint scheme, or blower scoop, or some such; seat is an old hot rod survivor that is the only un-stealth part of the car!

From top to bottom: This could have been in any 1956 driveway, but the cat would have to have been someone with a job, no?; early Chevy and four-speed make this car a tourer. Period is still correct, since car was "built" in '56, as a qualifier for River City Reliability Run; dropped axle, tube shocks, drum brakes.

his own man when it comes to his iron, though. While graybeard advice is taken to heart, independent decisions are then made. Result? The Stealth gear grabber in the attached photos. And black wheels on a black car. That takes courage. Black wheels let the whole image subtle-down; it's one of the ultimate "I won't do anything distracting from the overall look of this piece just to please someone else" statements you can make. If you have confidence in the package, it is sometimes distracting to "over-feature" some piece of it.

I'm OK. My rod's OK.

The coupe got lit for the first time about a day before Paso Robles, and you know what THAT means, doncha? Yeah. Break this bad boy in on the highway. About a 600-mile weekend proved they had gotten it right; and Brent's club, The Auto Butchers, celebrated with him appropriately at the event. But back to that break-in ride. Haven't you done it? Haven't you wondered if it was going to stay cool? Haven't you wondered if the oil was going to stay in it? If you had packed the wheel bearings enough? If all the suspension parts were working out? If the gas gauge was right? What kind of mileage you were getting? If you LOOKED cool?

That anxiety is part of the project. It's part of the reward.

Ask Brent Bell. He beat the demons of hot rod building and is thrashing his hot iron all over So Cal as we speak.

Hop Up Honor. Stay Honor.

GUNAR'S SHORT

Text & Photography by Jon Gobetti

Gunar Hansken has a quick wit and enough charm to easily separate you from your NOS (neat old stuff). As a member of the Swanx of Vallejo, California, he's helped other members build their rides. And Gunar knows how to build 'em on a tight budget.

The Swanx car club dates back to 1952. The older members mentor the young, teaching them skills they learned from years of building rods and customizing cars. Members help each other with their projects. It doesn't matter who possesses what skills or equipment. The year, make or model of their cars doesn't matter, either. What does matter? Building cars, sharing knowledge, and developing lifelong friendships. The end results are attractive, well-constructed, traditional rods, built on budgets ranging from $5,000 to $30,000.

Though Gunar's pickup is definitely at the lower end of that cost range, it's no less a hot rod than what you might find on the pages of *Rod & Custom* or *Street Rodder*. Gunar's short began with the boxing of Deuce rails and progressed with the installation of a 350/350 combination that transfers torque to the rear wheels through a Chevelle 12-bolt third member.

Upon these rails Gunar and company mounted an eclectic collection of Model B and 40 parts. The sum total of a back of a '34 cab, the top of a '33 pickup, and the cowl of a '32 make up the completed cab. The doors are of a questionable Ford vintage but lie within the years previously stated. The top was chopped in 1976 and sat on the deserted Mare Island submarine base for some time before Gunar rescued it and put it to proper use. He purchased the firewall from a young man without a clue, a deal that did not require the "Gunar charm" we warned you about. The '32 bed, found in Rio Vista, California, was properly shortened 17 inches with the wheel well arches remaining over the tires.

This low-dollar project was completed with a Mexican blanket interior, DuPont purple toner primer, and the skillful, steady hand of Ralph "Moochie" Finley, who picked up the horsehair and laid down the stripes.

All this in time (3:00 a.m.) for Andy's Picnic in 1996. Gunar has not stopped spinning the odometer since.

If you cut 'em up, you should begin with a body like this one. Gunar rescued and pieced together four different bodies to create his rod.

From left to right: Nothing fancy here. The 350 small-block runs six twos with the internals left stock for reliability; '40 Ford brakes with Buick drums and aftermarket air scoops provide ample stopping power for the lightweight rod; the simple interior is definitely low-dollar, yet fully functional. Gunar monitors engine vitals via five SW gauges nestled in the Deuce dash; the car on the Swanx plaque is a '51 Kaiser!

Legend & Rumor

THE BILL JERRY ROADSTER

Text by Peter T. Bennett
Photos by Peter T. Bennett & Walter Dupont

On a fine spring day in 1954, a 16-year-old Maine lad named Walter was on the road in search of a rumor. The noise was that, at a certain service station 35 miles or so from home, was a hot rod. A real hot rod, not just some '50 Ford gussied up for show.

The Calso station was exactly where he was told it would be, and under the overhang was not one, but two hot rods, a pair of channeled '32 Ford roadsters, in bright paint and with built motors, polished aluminum and loads of chrome, '40 dashes, boat windshields and finished interiors. An hour or two, maybe three, slipped by as Walter circled around with so many questions. He gathered himself up, took a half a dozen photos and somehow drove himself home. He would return many times that summer.

Those roadsters belonged to the station's owner and his chief mechanic, Bill Jerry. The cars had and would generate many rumors, folklore and eventually legend. Ham Allen's metallic blue roadster was started shortly after World War II and continued to evolve until the late '50s, when it was sold off and disappeared. Bill's metallic green roadster, with its bright yellow interior, would also evolve and disappear. These cars were built with two things in mind—speed and beauty. They were raced on the road and off. Bill would become a charter member of NHRA in 1951, and he pursued drag racing with a vengeance.

Speed! To that end a year's wages went into gathering parts for the big motor. "For a year all my money went to California," Bill said in a recent conversation. Racing pistons, a stroker crank, a wild cam, a dago-ed axle and more would all arrive on the Railway Express truck. The hot rod became faster and its reputation grew.

One of the stories that would reach epic proportions was the day the hot rods raced the Staties. One afternoon a state police captain arrived at the station with their newest pursuit car and suggested a test. At the edge of town was a two-mile stretch that would afford the captain his opportunity. It would be Bill this day in his green roadster as Ham's was down. "I'll give you a quarter of a mile jump, run her up good, and I'll pull you over," offered the captain. That was

Above: The Bill Jerry roadster was built in Maine in 1951. The Deuce was channeled 6-plus inches over the frame with a 6-inch Z in the rear. An adjustable rear spring perch allows for ride height changes. **From left to right:** On Walter's first visit, he photographed Bill Jerry's '50s-built roadster on the left and Ham Allen's '40s-built on the right; this 1954 photo shows the car in race trim. It was painted a '52 Plymouth metallic green with an extra handful of metallic added. The car was loud, fast and hard to miss.

Those are '46 Ford taillights, Hollywood Accessory plate light and mid '30s lights on the deck lid. No latch but 20 or so pounds of lead along the lower edge.

the last the trooper saw of Bill that day. A week or so later the captain, with his boss, arrived at the station to look into improving the performance of their fleet. The story has it that the captain said something to the effect of, "If I ever catch you...." Bill, after a long pause returned, "You won't."

Walter hung around the station, and one day his persistence paid off. "Hey kid, you want to go for a ride?" There was a new intake that needed a test. And 45 years later, Walter is still vibrating from the thrill. Had it not been for Walter's determination to see a real hot rod, and his photos, those roadsters would have remained just a rumor.

Bill Jerry continued to improve his roadster, and he remained competitive right up until the day he parked it. It stayed in moth balls until his son neared driving age. After much consideration he sold the car out of town. Fast-forward to 1972. Bill now has his own shop, and the young mechanic working for him was looking for a street rod project. "Look so-and-so up down the way, I'll bet he still has my old hot rod." A deal was struck, but years before it had been bricked up in a basement. The new owner, with the help of a friend, dismantled the car and carried it, a piece at a time, out a small door.

The new owner returned the roadster to the road in primer, with a fresh flathead and a rudimentary interior, and he drove it for 10 years or so. By all accounts it was never babied. On a cold November day during hunting season, he and a pal took the roadster deer hunting. They bagged a buck, laid it over the deck lid, and homeward they went. The car with its trophy, and a recently installed new motor with no anti-freeze, suffered from its exposure. The motor was frozen. The car was parked for years and the rumors began.

Fast-forward again to 1995. There was a persistent rumor that an old-timey channeled hot rod that had been in storage for nearly 20 years was surfacing once again. The previous owner had passed away, the widow was left with the car, and she was putting it up for bids.

Walter's six photographs would be instrumental in researching the car and finding the original owner. With the aid of Bill Jerry's keen memory, many of the missing details fell into place, as did many wonderful stories. The current owner returned the hot rod to its '50s configuration, preserving as much of the physical history as possible. With that approach in mind, the paint wasn't stripped; the dent from the buck's rack wasn't pounded out, the thrash from the tire's chains left in place. The roadster was dismantled, the tired equipment was replaced, a fresh motor was added, and the running gear was rebuilt. Once again, the old hot rod is road-worthy and it is driven.

Found! '32 FORD CABRIOLET Missing 35 Years!

By Dave Simard

No, it's not a '32 roadster. This one's a cabriolet—typically overlooked by most hot rodders. The origin of this nice cabriolet is unsure. Built around 1950, it incorporated the best components of the time, with outstanding attention to proportions.

I first became aware of this '32 when a friend pointed out a photo of it in the 1955 Hartford, Connecticut Autorama program. The '32 was at that time owned by Al Berton of Connecticut. The description of the convertible in the program read as follows:

"A 1948 286cu. in. Mercury engine of over 200 HP moves this sleek one at better than 140 mph. The modified engine uses Harmon & Collins ignition, Belond headers, Weiand three-carb manifold and heads, working out a compression ratio of 10 to 1. 'Z'ed frame uses a 4-inch Dago axle along with aircraft shocks and all front suspension is chromed. An unusual feature is the use of Kinmont disc brakes. A Glen Hauser Carson top is a 4-inch chop, touching off a 20-coat metallic bronze paint job. Using luggage clasps, the hood and side panels are louvered. With a full compliment of Stewart Warner gauges, the car is valued at present at $3,000."

Wow. After reading this and looking closer at the single photo in the program, I figured this was no ordinary hot rod of the time. Closer inspection shows that besides the 4-inch chop, the windshield posts were leaned back and the door window frames were modified front and back. Custom hairpin radius rods allowed the front to sit right, plus a custom track-style grille guard was installed up front. The more you look the more you discover, and discover is the word!

I couldn't help but wonder, what happened to this rod? So I started digging and found out that Al sold the car around 1958 and lost track after that. No one I asked seemed to know where the '32 went. Then, last year a local dealer called describing a '32 he had purchased and wanted to sell. The description over the phone made me wonder—could this be? Turned out it *was* Al's convertible.

The car was complete except for engine and transmission. Once I got it home, I decided I must try again to contact Al Berton. Unfortunately, I discovered that Al had passed away, though his son Todd was able to provide another dozen photos of the '32.

It's believed Al purchased the '32 around 1952 from a dealer in San Antonio, Texas, where he was stationed in the service. Al repainted the car and brought it to Connecticut around 1954. The car changed hands twice after Al sold it in 1958. The car somehow ended up in Massachusetts, where it was parked for good in 1963.

The cabriolet was believed to have been built in California around 1948-1950. When first constructed, it was dark green with a green leather interior and Auburn dash panel. The front track grille displays the letter "E" in the center—typically the owner/builder's last initial—but who is Mr. "E" and where is he?

Maybe "E" just stands for excellent. We couldn't agree more! With a look like this, who needs a roadster?

Page 17: Al's cabriolet around the time he bought it in San Antonio, Texas (note the Texas dealer tag). From this angle you can see the Pontiac taillights, rear rolled pan, custom rear bars and lots of sparkling chrome. **Opposite page**: The cabriolet as it sat on the San Antonio dealer's lot where Al found it. Note the '32's three-piece louvered hood, chromed hairpins, laid-back windshield posts and Carson top. **From top to bottom**: The rod's original builder probably put his initial in the grille-guard, but his name has been lost over time; no one knows who posed with the '32, but it wasn't Al; 286-inch Merc flathead used a Weiand three-carb manifold and heads.

KEEPER OF THE FLAME

Text & Photos By Peter Vincent

The first thing you need to understand is that these photographs were taken in 1990, some 10-plus years ago. Dick Page was into the "nostalgia" movement before it was even a consideration. In fact, I have to say that Dick is one of the originals. With him it is not a question of fads or movements. It's just the way he is. He has a true sense of the roots, and there is a long history of his involvement in the hot-rod and custom-car culture.

I first saw the '32 two-door in the late 1980s, and it stood out, shining like a beacon in the middle of all those high-tech cars of the time. A glimpse of it left a lasting image in my mind. It was painted flat black, which Dick said, with a chuckle, was Sherwin Williams military anti-radar flat black paint used on aircraft nosecones.

Dick first tried to buy the two-door in 1959, finally getting the '32 15 years later from Curt Kendal with a trade of two non-runners for a total cash outlay of $800. In Dick's words, "The form you see here is not an attempt at a theme car. No fuzzy dice, blue dots or milled stuff. Just an old hot rod with some changes made along the way. A deliberate effort has been made to preserve the old flavor intact and to avoid using store-bought brackets and fad pieces."

The only current photograph in the group. Dick Page's '32 two-door as it is today, Denny Hall's roadster pickup and a '51 Merc custom project that Dick is working on for Denny.

From the top: The fit of tires and fenders. Narrow front centered and rears covered by widened fenders; nothing profiles better than a chopped two-door that sits right.

This car has been driven. Dick put over 121,000 miles on the odometer before 1990. It was used as a street racer, daily driver, and even as a push-car for Art Chrisman's Hustler nostalgic dragster at one time. It is still being driven daily.

Dick chopped the top 3 inches in 1985, at which time the blower motor was also added. The '77 four-bolt 350 Chevy truck block and 4-71 GMC blower was topped off with a Predator 6000 carb and an old Hilborn air scoop left over from Dick's high school days. The blower is today topped with dual fours. Hot rods, being the evolutionary things that they are, constantly change. Early Hedman headers and a Mallory dual-point distributor help it all come together. The original, non-rebuilt radiator runs at 180 degrees with the addition of a manually switched electric fan. Dick mentioned that he did add three tubes of stop-leak to the radiator. A Pro-Stock 'Glide from Lakewood Transmission and an Art Carr converter are still in use and run by a B&M cable shifter. The rearend is a Ford 9-inch with 4.10s and a locker.

Original framerails were used with a Model A front crossmember. The front spring eyes have been reversed, and a 1950s Stewart dropped axle is in place with stock magnafluxed spindles. The split wishbones and framerails have been notched for steering clearance, which Dick believes to be much stronger than heating and bending steering arms. Plus the full turning radius is maintained. The front tie rod has been dropped in the center to clear the blower drive, with gussets added at the bends to stiffen the unit. He says everything has survived all the high-speed chuckholes. He also added a VW steering dampener to help eliminate road shock. The front brakes are out of a '64 Ford truck, and the rears are '75 Ford wagon units.

The wide-white 820/15 Bruce cheater slicks are mounted on swap meet chrome wheels with the centers painted to cover the rust. Non-reversed front wheels keep the 600/15 tires centered under the fenders.

The interior is virtually non-existent. The rear seat is a recovered stock unit, and the fronts are out of a '65 Mustang. The column drop is a 1940 Moon unit, and all gauges are Stewart Warner units. There is no headliner, and the door panels are bare hardboard painted flat black. The tape deck is dead, and the gas gauge hasn't worked for 15 years.

At one time the car won "best unfinished" at a local rod run. Dick gave the award back and told them it was finished. A rather vocal editor of a national association's news publication was overheard by a friend of Dick's saying something to the effect that, "Owners of these damn nostalgia cars don't do a thing to support the street rod industry. All you guys do is comb the swap meets looking for bargains. You're all just going along for the free ride." We prefer to think of it as being keepers of the flame. Oh yeah, total cash spent as of the summer of 1990 was still under $3,000.

The '32 has since evolved some more with different tires and wheels and the afore-mentioned dual fours on top of the blower. But it looks great as ever and is still being used.

From the top: View of the 4-71 blower, Predator carb (which has been replaced with dual fours) and that nice Hilborn topper; this '32 looks good from any angle; wide white 820/15 Bruce cheater slicks.

Dick Brown's '41 Ford custom, looking to all the world as if just rolled out of the late '40s. Straight, black and with the correct angle of attack.

Homemade taillights, a smooth fit and finish, all the body-lines coming together at the bustle.

The '50 Merc motor was bored, stroked and fitted with Navarro heads, a Thickston intake, Howard M7 cam, tube headers and tons of chrome.

he office: Light brown rolls and pleats, tons of chrome on
ne dash, column, garnish moldings. That's a '46 Ford
eluxe wheel, working radio, and working record player.

THE WAY THEY WERE

Text & Photos By Peter T. Bennett

Where does the vision to radically alter an otherwise mundane car come from? When we asked Dick Brown how he chose to build his '41 Ford custom, he told us, "I wanted something old, no billet, 350s, or clips. You know, the way they were. You remember that club that Barris built all the identical '41s for? That's the look. The old speed boat coming up out of the water, noise high, throttling forward with the sound of expensive horsepower as it comes to speed. That's the right stuff."

Before Dick found it, the '41 had been abandoned in central New England. Left to the weather for years with no top and partially taken apart, it was now waiting to go to the crusher, the last car in the lot behind a derelict service station. Dick found the car after it was already put on the trailer—none too soon—and saved it.

When the '41 came off the ramp truck into his garage, Dick took time to really go over his new project. With careful canvassing of the hulk the to-do list grew. The floor was gone, the deck lid was caved, the fenders were junk and the running boards weren't much better. And then there was the rust. With winter coming a decision needed to be made.

At a local swap meet, Dick put photos on a board with the intention of moving the old hulk. The first pass through the swap meet produced an NOS deck lid for short money. At least it would bulk up the sale. On his way out of the gate, a friend asked if he had seen the running boards. There, still in the factory wrapping were two brand new '41 Ford running boards! Slowly the romance was rekindled.

Driving home with his prizes, Dick allowed for a detour through his old neighborhood, and something nagged at him. One summer night, 40-plus years ago, on this tree-lined street, as a bicycle-riding kid, he encountered a vision. At first he couldn't make it out. Unlike anything he had ever seen before it seemed to glide out of the dark, rumbling as it came towards him. The light flashing on the bar of the ripple disk had an ever-increasing hypnotic effect. Slowly moving from shadow to light, coming ever closer, this black fluid image revealed itself. It was a chopped and channeled '39 Ford custom.

As his head cleared from the old vision, he realized this one would be black too, and he began to map out the work necessary to save the old carcass. The body shell was stripped of its remaining parts and sent to the sand blaster. The frame, with its now flattened rear crossmember, was sandblasted and painted, the first customizing. A new floor was made, and a kick-up was built in the trunk to house the altered crossmember. The local auto hunter and *Hemmings* turned up four NOS fenders and a nearly perfect hood. With the new sheet metal hung in place it was beginning to get the look. At this point his attention turned to the drivetrain, and he installed a radical flat motor. Most of the drivetrain was either new or rebuilt, and again he went looking for a body shop. Across town was a kid who wanted to do the car. So across town the car went, to be chopped and have a few patch panels added. Again the work slowed and the car was pushed to a corner, and again it was time for the car to come home.

The car now sat for many months while Dick looked for someone to complete the bodywork. At some point he was introduced to Dave Simard at East Coast Custom, and they talked about the car. Dave took the body back to bare metal, removed the Bondo repairs and cut it in half through the doors to correct the door gap. He also made the center grille piece and joined the hood. Both were works of art. The Winfield Carson top was cut and stretched and made to fit the 5-inch chop. All the stainless trim was cut, welded, and metal finished.

While the car was at Simard's, Dick retired, moved and resettled with a new, almost empty garage. He brought the '41 home. Now he had nothing but time to devote to this project. He wired the car, installed the chrome dash and instruments, and mounted the Buick solenoids for the doors and trunk. The garnish moldings were sent out and chromed along with countless small parts. He contracted a local body shop to paint the car, black of course. Shortly the top was covered in white and the trunk and interior upholstered in a light brown.

Dick, a stickler for details, had for years been collecting the right parts, real Appletons and accessory hubcaps. The parts that didn't meet his level of finish were stripped and rechromed. Finding the right period outside mirrors took countless trips to swap meets and many phone calls. He crafted the Lucite taillights over a buck he carved himself, and formed them in the kitchen stove. "That's the way they did it," he would often say. All the pieces were finally in one place, the details ironed out, and the custom was now finished.

So what moves a person to take on a car that took nearly five years to complete? For Dick, the way they were had been burned into his memory nearly 50 years ago on a hot summer night. Recently on a rare outing with the black custom, he was asked, "Why?" "I built it for me, because that's the way it was."

Keith Ashley's '51 BEL AIR

It was the 50th: The Golden Anniversary of the Oakland Roadster Show or whatever the pundits, courts and mags and rod/custom PC monitors have decided to call it.

It was Oakland.

We had done what we usually do: Flew up to SFO; got picked up by three hairy-legged hot rod types with car prevarication, laughs and beer on their minds; and went to "move in" at the show. It always feels like an inside line around the track—an in-crowd deal. You may not know everybody there, but being there watching them do the final wipe-down and set up the last velvet rope makes you feel like part of the creative process. It's better, though, because you don't have the stress and hard work that all the exhibitors have. And it's a great way to spend the day, being with pals who are equally as opinionated (read: snob-rodders) and performing the requisite ad hoc judging duties. You cats do it too, no?

After pacing around the main floor and greeting some pals, I took a stroll toward the main entry and, not knowing that it was being prepped for the Barris Tribute, stumbled onto Matranga (copy), Hirohata (restored), a couple of others, and then kinda got bumped out of the way by some stovebolt-sounding sled that was pulling in. Must be delivering some angel hair, huh? Sure enough, it was an Inliner—and it was slammed and it was Fifties tri-colored to scare the bejezus out of ya. And, whoa daddy! It's the Ernst car! I reached for Rustman to tell him about my discovery and found I was there alone, surrounded by a

Top to bottom: The cat in this car woulda got the chicks, right?; Ashley took a few tasteful liberties in the remake of the original; Ashley custom along with Ernst and Bradley cars made for a nice Bel Air feature last summer.

bunch of hicks I didn't know milling around trying to block my stinkin' view of my favorite car in the whole world! Where's the rest of the River City guys, man? They gotta see this. I did, finally, get a long, close look at the car, and picked up from some better-informed (hick) person that it was a copy of the second iteration of the Ernst car, from the garage of Keith Ashley.

What a cool job, Keith. What a mellow short.... Keith had seen the original at his high school about an eon ago. Figure it: It was on the cover of *Hot Rod* in '53 and won the *Motor Life* (what *Hop Up* became when it grew up) Most Beautiful Custom of the Year in '54. Yes, it was a few summers ago, amigos mios. So that is the image that got Keith started on his long road to automotive excess (say hallelujah, Brothers). And that is why, while he's not the cat who got to restore the original one, he's still got his Chevy done his way. See, Keith's version approximates the car in its second life. It had been remade once, he dug that version and—as we'll see—made subtle improvements. We at *Hop Up* feel that a tribute car like this is WAY more "Ashley" than "Ernst." It'd be different, of course, if the in-the-tin original was the subject, but it wasn't. It was some bone-ass stocker that Keith Ashley saved for himself and for the pleasure of Hop Up Guys all over the US of A.

This car has been featured by some of the best of them, and although we don't like to "cover" feature cars, we feel it's our own since the Ernst car was in *Hop Up* in 1952 and Keith is a Hop Up Guy. Thus we won't belabor all the mods that make the car so special. The liberties taken in the design of the hardtop were inspired, tasteful, and enhance the project in the custom way: Each element contributes to the whole, and doesn't stand alone as an aesthetic feature. Each touch was made to soften the look and make things fit and flow, resulting in the car's striking profile.

Harry Bradley was commissioned to maximize the great-for-the Fifties design. The grille, grille teeth, bumpers, bumper guards, Continental kit, skirts and side-scoop teeth all got something from today to make them work better without looking Baroque, like some multi-feature customs from the Fifties do.

Keith's letter to us concludes, "...the completion of this car fulfills a 45-year dream, and the next dream is in the planning stages. Nuff said...."

What'll ya bet that dream ends up on these pages, too?

PHOTO BY KEITH ASHLEY

Top to bottom: Ashely car (right) is a handsome near-reflection of the restored original; dressed Stovebolt 6 looks good, sounds good, too; Hop Up's favorite customs are those with subtle mods that contribute to the overall illusion.

Graves

BAD TO THE BROUGHAM

Photos by Dain Gingerelli

Factory customs are the few cars that, but for a little ride-compromising slammin,' came out of the box as custom cars. Rivieras, tri-year Mercs, '54 Mercs, and, well, you know them all, don't you? The foremost of these must be the outrageous Cad Eldorado Brougham of the '50s, a loss-leader that cost more to build than they could ever recover from its sale. The Brougham was a design and production opportunity for the Cad Dads to try their hand at Continental-like eccentricity.

Richard Graves always wanted one. That's no stretch. Most Hop Up Guys want one of everything but haven't enjoyed the coincidence of planning and opportunity to make them all happen. But Richard builds cars for himself and for customers, finding in those efforts an expression of the way he would do each of the projects that he has coveted throughout his experience in the rod and custom world. There was no magic to the Cad. No mystical formula. No insight or innovation that required renderings and design meetings. But the execution had to be fine. Whoa!

What do you do with a car whose body was hand-built by Pininfarina and shipped on dollies to the U.S.? Nose, deck, lower, paint, plate, trim and rim. But the work has to be fine. This was the highest-end car available in the 1958 US of A. The bumpers are polished aluminum. The gravel guards are polished stainless steel. The top is, of

Top: Cross pollination of American/Italian designs made a certain statement: Luxo-livery. **Bottom from left to right:** Maybe the best fin treatment of the '50s. Things went pretty haywire elsewhere in '58 and flat out WILD in '59!; Cadillac interior didn't need much improvement. Whitey Morgan finessed black leather over stock fixtures for the perfect look of elegance; E.V. cranked out limited edition 17's for the Brougham; Richard's traditional red steelies had to get a pass this time!!

course, brushed stainless.

Black urethane enamel went on in Richard's shop; black leather was stretched, pleated, seamed and stitched by Whitey Morgan; a '65 Cad 429 and Turbo 400 trans went in with the stock rear end; the abandoned air ride (upgraded to conventional coil suspension as a dealer upgrade) was conventionally lowered; the Old Cold (air) was re-charged, and then the talk with E. Rick Vaughn to collaborate on a set of custom 17x8-inch Real Wheels with custom-machined centers featuring genuine Cad medallions. And voila!

R.G. turned the car up somewhat by accident, and brought it in on spec—on speculation that it would become a customer car, probably. That all changed when he rolled the project over in his mind, visualized the results (ya gotta have vision, right?) and concluded he'd have time to do this one for himself. The more the plan was refined, the more eager he and his crew were to get started. Their enthusiasm translated to fine execution of a basic plan, results of which can be seen here in Dain's photo work.

Enjoy a feast for the eyes on *Hop Up!* ...

Top to bottom: Black on black in black, with stainless and aluminum accents; go ahead. Measure it...it's gotta be at least 25 feet long; aluminum bumpers are a throwback to cast aluminum (firewalls, floorboards) of the classic era.

The BATMOBILE

A '50s Star Makes A Comeback

Text & Photography by Jon Gobetti

Historically, the San Francisco Bay Area has had a pervading influence on America's custom car culture. There was a time in the East Bay when candy and pearl were the preferred finishes for coating the extravagant metalwork of the masters. Joe Wilhelm, Joe Ortega, Gordon Vann, Gene Winfield, Tommy the Greek and the Barris brothers were a few of the reigning masters of that craft. Few today realize that Bailon and the Barris brothers got their start in the San Joaquin Valley, which lies just over the hills from the San Francisco Bay.

Since the early 1950s, the Swanx Car Club has also been part of that same mystique. Ted Lundquist, who at one time worked with George Barris, started the Oakland chapter in 1952. The Vallejo chapter began in late 1953. The original 14 members held their meetings at Ted's shop/home in Oakland. Today's member roster totals 17.

The Batmobile, an original club car, was

purchased as a stock, burned-out '56 Oldsmobile 88. Its reincarnation began in 1957 by Neb Neblett and his son Al. Neb owned Vallejo Body Works in Vallejo, California, a small town just north and across the bay from Oakland. Al worked there after school and on weekends.

Returning from a late afternoon lunch, Neb found that Al had cut the top of the Olds. As the owner of a body shop, Neb could expect nothing less from his own blood. "That's my boy!" So began the father and son's transformation of the Oldsmobile into a custom car. They soon had the body dechromed and the headlights frenched. Deciding that was just not quite enough, the duo peaked the tops of the front fenders. The hood was then punched with five rows of 20 louvers. Tail fins from a '57 Chrysler were grafted to the quarter panels and fitted with a set of custom lenses. When completed, the fins looked like bat wings to both Neb and Al. They dubbed the Oldsmobile the "Bat-Mobile." Get it? A single antenna was frenched and sunken into the driver's-side front fender, and the grille cavity was filled with a '53 Chevy grille bar and extra teeth.

With all the cosmetic modifications completed, the body was prepped and coated with pearl white and accented with candy blue scallops. Final touches included '58 Impala side spears that replace the original stainless trim, a pair of Appleton spots and full-length lake pipes. They lowered the suspension 5 inches. A set of chromed rims with wide whitewalls completed the body modifications.

Inside they finished the seats and package tray in white tuck-and-roll, and a black wool carpet complemented the two-tone exterior. The original dash was left unmolested except for custom knobs.

Today, the Batmobile does little to hide its middle age. However, under the stewardship of present owner Paul Grilli, the Batmobile has found a loving home. In 1960,

Opposite page, from the top: In profile, the '58 Impala side spear and Chrysler tail fins are very recognizable. It's also very apparent that this '56 Olds 88 is a four-door; the '57 Chrysler tail fins are filled with custom-made lenses; the original grille has been filled with a '53 Chevrolet grille bar and extra teeth; **This page, from the top:** This angle emphasizes the frenched headlights and peaked fenders; the package tray is also covered in white tuck-and-roll.

From the top: From a distance, the Batmobile hides its age well. The father-and-son team of Neb and Al Neblett transformed the burned-out hulk into a stunning custom in 1957; traditional white tuck-and-roll pleats cover both front and rear bench seats. Paul replaced the original worn-out carpet with black wool.

Paul's friend Keith Whittaker wrecked his '56 Corvette and took it to Vallejo Body Works for an estimate. Rather than repairing the Vette, he ended up trading it for the Batmobile. He and Paul cherish the days they spent cruising their local haunts in the custom. Soon the three would take different paths. Paul entered the Army, and Keith and the Olds went their separate ways.

Today, after a long search, Paul has been reunited with the Batmobile. He now cherishes both old memories and the pink slip. In an effort to stop the aging process, Paul replaced the windshield, which was cracked back in 1961. (It took four attempts to cut down a single windshield to replace the original.) He also replaced the carpet and worn-out rubber. He rechromed where necessary and replaced the tired old power plant with a rebuilt '56 Olds engine and Jet-Away transmission.

The old pearl and candy paint has been touched up here and there. Paul feels a new paint job would ruin the mystique of this original Fifties classic custom car. We couldn't agree more.

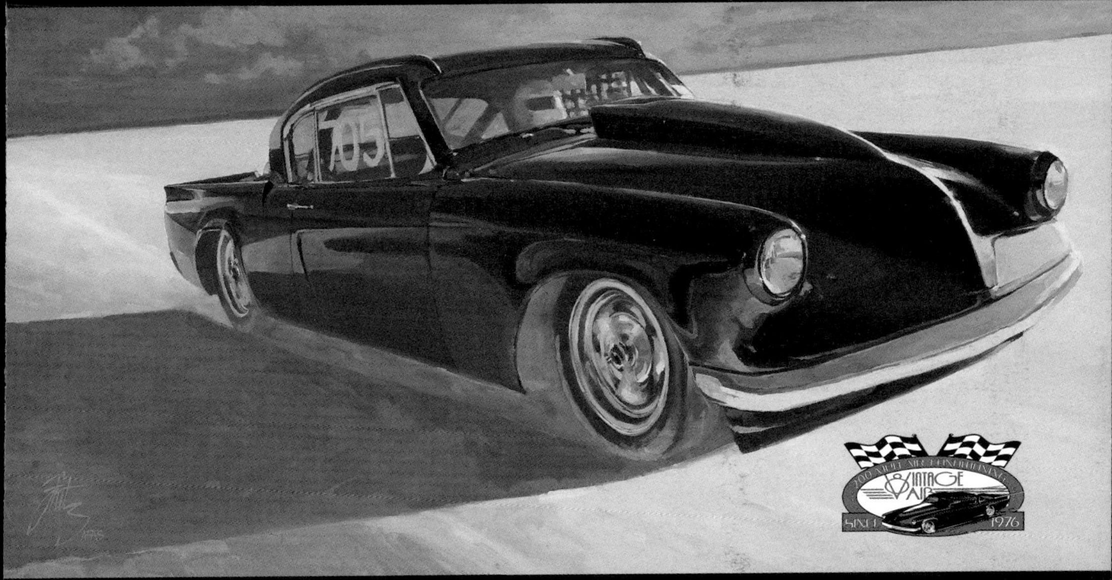

Why do we do this thing called hot rodding?

To push the performance envelope?

To test our abilities and skills?

To make our products the best they can be?

To be a part of an American tradition?

Yes.

VINTAGE AIR

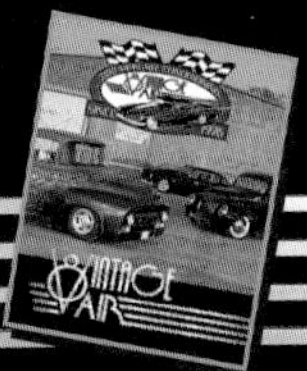

The Most Respected Name In Performance Air Conditioning
Call 800.862.6658 for a catalog or for your nearest dealer

There seems to be a contest to see which publication can score the most neat, unseen, old-timey rodding photos, and scoop everybody else. Here at the Hop Up Towers, we can't go out and brown-nose and suck-up like some of them do—we got jobs—so we have to take advantage of the favors of Hop Up Guys who, only because we speak more rodding truth than any of the rest of them, have chosen us to publish their unobtanium photos.

These resources may dry up someday (naaaaaw!), so lean back. Savor them, and dream about all that might have surrounded the cropped shots that follow—engines revving in the background, buddies yelling at one another, "Ford for gow! Chevy for plow!" Imagine how really cool Tommy the Greek was, cruising Nor-Cal in his '36, an iconoclast then, an iconoclast now. Go back with us in time (didn't they say that in the Lone Ranger?) and study…dissect these foggy images. If you are keen of wit and keen of eye, you may pick up some design clue that the rest of us had forgotten...or never known…and you can employ it in the pursuit of hot rod happiness.

en hopup veritas

PHOTO COURTESY DAVID SIMON COLLECTION

TOMMY THE GREEK

PHOTO STOLEN BY STROUPE

On the occasion of his 86th birthday, a hundred or so of Tommy the Greek's closest friends came together to celebrate. The event was covered by the monthly magazine world, but the legend of the striper has overshadowed the reality that began with a rod/custom guy in the Thirties. The photo here is of Tommy's '36 phaeton, probably taken in '37 or '38. Hop Up Guy Frank McFadden remembers the car around Oakland at the time. Mac was younger—he says a "tot" but we're not believin' it—and remarks that it was among only three or four standout cars in the area. The Greek was definitely a Big Dog in the car world already. Good taste and budget can do that for ya.

The custom was black and at one time had white scallops with baby blue "Greek" stripes. It was adorned with the gee-gaws of the day, some of which still work in our traditional rod and custom community today. Skirts, single-bar Flippers with 'rings, Buick steering wheel, a tarp over the rear passenger compartment, spare tire relocated lower, custom hood panels and, well, you can see how cool the thing was in the picture. We think the car later got a Duvall windshield and a custom "Carson"-type top by Cal Hall, which indemnifies the fact that there were some cool and tasteful design treatments being done long before the late Forties.

DEAN BATCHELOR

...really was the "Dean."

He was a hot rodder/motorsport aficionado whose youth was wasted—like yours—messing about with old cars. Although he spent years in the sporty and classic car world, he was a hot rodder at the core. Again, like you.

And me.

Batchelor shared his beginnings with the hot rod and custom publishing world, most notably as Editor of *Hop Up* Magazine. He had the sense and organizational ability to accumulate a photographic archive—a lifetime photographic archive—of his time. He croaked in the mid-Nineties, and the archives went to Ron Kellogg, from whom we got the photos in this section. Many of these images (including our 2001 cover) are the original prints or negatives used in the original *Hop Ups* at that time. Pretty cool.

ALL PHOTOS BATCHELOR ARCHIVES/RON KELLOG COLLECTION

Opposite page, clockwise from top: Reg Schlemmer's '27 T was *Hot Rod* magazine's first cover car, though Batchelor shot it from a different angle than Pete; Bert Letner's modified roadster on the lakes in 1947; Ralph Poole caught Howard Johansen's Twin Tank in 1949. How many of those official SCTA jackets are still around? **From top to bottom**: Two views of the stunning John Gerraghty '40 Ford custom built by Gil Ayala and shot by Ralph Poole in 1952; prep for a run at the Russetta dry lakes meet in June, 1952.

If you have copies of the little R&Cs, you may recall Bob McNeil's "Lonesome" three-window from its July 1954 feature, written from the '32's point of view by Lynn Wineland and photographed by Ralph Poole. McNeil finished the coupe in a black and white motif, accenting the black lacquer with a white plastic insert in the chopped top, white rubber on the running boards and wide whites all around. "I thought Bob was just on some kind of a kick with this color business," wrote the coupe. "But he must have known what he was up to, 'cause when we pulled into the drive-in, I was the center of attraction. I was pronounced as being cool, mellow, cute and even something called 'Zorch.' Is that good?" Bumpers were from a '41 Ford, taillights from a '41 Chevy, and new sealed beams were set on a reshaped and rechromed lightbar. Chuck Porter's Body Shop chopped the top 3 1/2 inches, filled the cowl vent and grille, louvered the hood and shot the lacquer. Under that louvered hood was a '50 Merc flathead with Edelbrock heads and dual-carb manifold, Weber 3/4 cam and Mallory ignition. A '48 Merc tranny sent power down shortened driveshafts to a '40 Ford rearend. So why was this sweet coupe called Lonesome? McNeil had to park the car in March of '54 to go into the service. "I know Bob has big plans for me when he gets back in a year or two, and I can hardly wait," the coupe wrote. Wonder what those big plans were, and where this gorgeous car is now?

ALL PHOTOS BATCHELOR ARCHIVES/RON KELLOG COLLECTION

1932-34 FORD CHASSIS

Highboy or Fendered
Boxed Rails
Forged Axle • 9" Rear
Tube X • 4 Bar or
Hairpin Radius Rods
Flatheads, 5-Speeds

AS LOW AS **$4995.00**

32 Ford Chassis

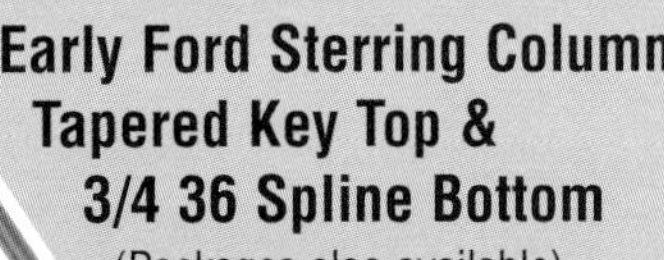

Early Ford Sterring Column
Tapered Key Top &
3/4 36 Spline Bottom
(Packages also available)

T-5 to Flathead Trans Kit

FLATHEAD FANS

Take Your Flathead Into the 21st Century
Chevy waterpump conversion kit. Stock biscuit or custom urethane bushed mounts. Add our CNC machined 8BA style timing cover with the T-5 overdrive conversion and fuel injection.

Buggy Spring Rear Suspension & Custom 1928-40 Ford Chassis Are No Problem!

RR 1 Box 47, Alexandria, NE 68303

VISA **(402) 749-1932 Fax (402) 749-1933**

email: gm03319@navix.net

GLENDALE
Sidewinders
2
Sta-Lube

WORLD'S FASTEST HOT ROD

By Tony Thacker

Over 50 years ago, two young hot rodders proved that if you wanted to go fast, streamlining—enclosing the wheels and axles—was the way to go. Of course, Dean Batchelor and Alex Xydias weren't the first lakes racers to realize this. In 1939, the Spaulding Brothers, Bill and Tom, took their so-called "Carpet Sweeper" to the dry lakes. With an ungainly body made of steel and a near stock 21-stud Ford flathead V8, it ran an uninspiring 131 mph—barely any faster than contemporary highboy roadsters. The concept was ignored.

In Europe, there were numerous streamliners setting speed records, not least of which were the Mercedes and Auto Unions. But details of their achievements barely filtered down to the hot rodders of Southern California. Besides, they were big-engined or big-buck efforts.

After World War II, the hot rod scene changed dramatically. Many of the young racers were now trained aircraft mechanics. They knew something of tuning and they understood the principles of slippery shapes. Bill Burke, a member of the Road Runners, might have been the first to take a

surplus 165-gallon-capacity P-51 wing tank, add wheels to the corners, drop in an engine and go fast—131.96 in 1946. Others, including Jack Avakian, Arnold Birner and Alex Xydias, were quick to follow, but it was Xydias' So-Cal Speed Shop Special that would make an impression.

The same day he was discharged from the Army Air Corps, where he worked as a B-17 engineer, the young Xydias borrowed some money and opened a small speed shop on Olive Avenue in Burbank. He was quick to understand the need to prove himself and the equipment he sold, so he assembled the tank using a Ford Model T frame and a '39 V8-60 engine fitted with Edelbrock heads and manifold, a Winfield cam and Spalding ignition. Built by Bobby Meeks and producing about 145 horsepower, the combination proved successful. In August 1948, it took the Class A record at 130.155 mph.

Over the winter of '48 Alex teamed up with Dean Batchelor, who had been studying automotive aerodynamics and German efforts in particular. They removed the belly tank and narrowed the front and rear track to 48 inches. The frame was then taken to Neil Emory's Valley Custom Shop in Burbank, where they hand beat a new aluminum body.

There was not enough time for the wheel covers to be finished, so the streamliner's first runs were made at El Mirage with the wheels exposed and the body devoid of paint. Nevertheless, the car fared well enough to complete the bodywork, paint it gold and white, and make the 700-mile trek to Bonneville.

At that first Bonneville Nationals in August 1949, they were the hit of the meet and created American automotive history. However, they were not alone. Lee Chapel, another speed shop owner, had Bob Allinger beat him out a shape that closely resembled the un-tried Mercedes record machine of 1939. Chapel also made a run before Bonneville but his engine was out of tune. Batchelor and Xydias clocked a two-way average of 156.39 mph—much faster than the belly tank had ever gone—giving them a

Class A record. Not bad for an engine down to only about 110-115 horsepower due to the 4,200-foot elevation.

There was more to come though. Standing by was Bobby Meeks with a potent, full-race, 275-cubic-inch Merc V8 set up for Class C records. This motor was dropped into the 'liner, and Dean clocked a one-way of 193.54 mph. His two-way average was 189.745. On this last run the treads peeled away from the front tires, but the car remained stable.

Over the winter, the V8-60 was put back into the 'liner and the two young men returned to El Mirage. After an impressive run of 152 mph, Batchelor turned around for the return run into the wind. Some reports say he became airborne and literally flew over the 132-foot timing traps. That was not the case, according to Alex Xydias. A combination of luck, safety belts and sturdy body construction saved Dean as he rolled once and came to a standstill right side up. It took the rest of the season to beat out the dents, though.

By August the car was rebuilt and quickly finished in black primer. The team returned to Bonneville but with Bill Dailey and Ray Charbonneau sharing the driving. Again, they were not alone. Lee Chapel returned, and there were new streamliners from Bill Kenz and Marvin Lee—all determined to break records. Experience proved its worth, though, and the So-Cal team pushed the Class A record to 162.95 with the V8-60.

The twin-engined Kenz car was hot on their tail and gained a Class D record. Sadly, Lee's "City of Pasadena" car, driven by Puffy Puffer, flipped at around 200 mph, bounced on its top, flew 156 feet and made a few more loops before Puffy emerged with a bruised ear.

The So-Cal team went out again, this time with the mighty Merc installed. They set new Bonneville and Class C records of 208.927 on a two-way run over a measured mile, with a fastest time of 210.92 mph and a quarter mile one-way run of 211.227—setting a new all-time record for American cars. Streamlining was suddenly the only way to go if you wanted to go fast.

A 1934 FORD GOW WAGON

By Albert Drake

At mid-century, when I began reading new magazines such as *Hop Up*, *Honk!* and *Hot Rod*, I knew little about cars, and yet occasionally I saw a feature on a car that I somehow sensed had a history. But those pieces were generally limited to photos and captions, and there was no room in which to trace a car's history if it had one. Besides, the editors wanted to create the impression that every car was new and fresh; nostalgia is a term that has gained currency during the past decade.

But another reason for omitting a car's history is because getting the facts is often difficult work. Sometimes it's impossible to trace a modified car back over the years. You have to depend on primary sources, people who knew the car. Often the key people have moved or passed away.

Such seemed to be the case recently. A Portland rodder, Mike Kelly, gave me a copy of a photograph that he had bought in an antique store. He wondered about the car, a '34 Ford roadster, and he thought I might know something about it. I did not, but since I can well remember the couple of '34 Ford roadsters I saw during the 1950s, I felt that I should remember it.

The car had been lowered, the windshield had been chopped, and it had a neat custom top that appeared to fold. It had solid wheels (which indicated that the photo was taken after 1939); small, smooth hubcaps; a 1937 DeSoto rear bumper that appeared to have been raised, and a spare tire that had been lowered and laid parallel to the body line. The taillight(s) sat low and on a short stand, which suggested to Mike that the stock '34 light had been moved inboard to the gas tank cover. Mike also commented on the tight side curtains, the radio antenna and the dirty rear tire, all of which suggested that the roadster was used as daily transportation. And Mike noted the car's most distinctive feature—the 1936 Ford rear fenders and skirts, a neat touch that makes the car outstanding.

On the back of the photo was written "1943" and "'34 V-8 Gow Wagon," which got my heart beating because I took it as proof that guys did use that term. Except for a note saying that the writer had intended to put in the wood—referring to that pile in the driveway beyond the car—there was nothing to identify the owner of this "gow wagon."

The need to find out more about this car became a quest. There were so few 1933-'34 Ford roadsters, and that rear fender treatment was so distinctive, I was certain I'd find someone who knew the car. I showed the photo to all kinds of people, but had no luck. I hang out with some rodders and racers who are a few years older than I am, and I passed the photo around, but no one responded.

More than a year passed, and one day I delivered a book to Jack Lofton, a fellow I've known for several years. He was a rodder during the 1940s and '50s, but he's always been interested in boats. Over the decades he has built hundreds of them. He's got photo albums of nothing but boats. The album he handed me on this day had photos of his cars, though, and after a few pages there it was—not only the same '34 Ford roadster, but the same photo! There were other photos of it beside a river, and with a bunch of skiers on Mt. Hood. There were even a couple of early color prints, showing that the car at some point had been painted red.

Some things about the roadster were clear in Jack's mind. He had the car in 1943, and he did the work that appeared in the photo. The house in the background belonged to his parents; the small garage beyond the car was where he built a rear-engine belly tank for dragging in 1950, and a '29 A-V8 roadster in 1951. Beyond that his memory became a little unclear, not only because 55 years had passed, but also because he owned two '34 Ford roadsters about the same time. He thinks that the one in the photo is the one he drove to Yakima, Washington, for the roadster races and traded it for another car. If it is, he's certain that he never saw it again.

What's unclear in my mind is how all the people I showed the car to—many of them friends of Jack's over the years—claimed that they had never seen the car. Some of them must have ridden in it! Let this serve as incentive to anyone seeking to know a car's history: Just keep at it; the person who knows might be right around the corner.

Swap Meet

Hop Up asked some of its favorite, coolest guys to contribute something to this epochal piece of literature, and what they sent makes up the following chapter. They were not given specific topics or assignments. They were expected to do something righteous that might never appear in mainstream mags and, who'd-a-thought? They came through like the hairy-legged hot rod types they are. The result is a collage of interests and thoughts and history and how-tos and images and...well, ya just gotta read it for yourself.

We got great pals.

PHOTO COURTESY DAVID SIMON COLLECTION

STRAIGHT BL

George Fields taking off on the long course at Bonneville in 1999. This '37 Simca has reached speeds of 300-plus mph and holds records in more than one class. He has also left the ground at 300 mph, which is the reason for the new covered-wheel front end.

ACK & WHITE

Text & Photos By Peter Vincent

I should have titled this article

"A Subjective Justification of Black & White Photography." But, this is about hot rods, the landscape and the very natural interaction between the two. The photographs included were taken out on the dry lakes of Southern Cal or on the great white of the Bonneville salt. While I believe the same thoughts and perceptive values exist for both color and black & white photography, there is a fundamental difference on how they are viewed and perceived. Color is "natural" and what many have come to expect, especially when it helps define what is being photographed. For example, the red of a red car matters in a color photograph, and it can be a dominant design element within the image. I also believe that the composition and overall photographic design have a lot to do with whether or not it is a "good" photograph. The thing about color, for me, is that it can distract from the message, or information that I am trying to pass to the viewer. Black & white photography cuts directly to content and concept design elements to reach the viewer. Good color photography should also do the same thing.

What I am interested in is that which is beyond the automobile. It, or the image, becomes a spatial relationship between hot rods and the landscape. The formal visual elements and principles of design become dominant in the overall visual structure, and the image is reduced to only that which is necessary. Hopefully there are no distractions to wade through in a visual sense. The subject, or hot rod, is seen for what it is, and it becomes an integral part of the landscape. It belongs there and has a sense of drama, which is in keeping with what turns me on to the culture. It's edgy and direct, but it also keeps the viewer wondering (hopefully) and feeling a sense about time and place. This is going to sound a little off-beat, but bear with me because I'm going to say it anyway. Black & white photography is more difficult to pull off, because the formal design has to work. The more you reduce anything visual, the more precise the composition and subject orientation have to be in order to transfer meaningful information. Conversely, the more visual application you throw into an image, the more difficult it is to produce a meaningful photograph. Good black & white photography is difficult and good color photography is equally difficult. We just seem to accept color imagery at a lower perceptive level.

Why do I photograph various aspects of the hot rod culture in black & white? First, it has a lot to do with tradition. It is how I learned photography originally, when I was turned on to Adams and Weston images. The beautiful Adams' landscapes would not have the same effect, or drama, in color. The same thing holds with Edward and Brett Weston's black & white photographic

Page 56: This '29 roadster has been at the last two Muroc events, and I ran into it at Bonneville during Speedweek in 1999. **Page 57**:**Above**: This photograph of Brett Reed's '32 highboy, was taken in Wendover after an obvious day out on the "somewhat damp" salt. **Below (left to right)**: I photographed this '59 Caddy convertible at Bonneville in '98; Fabian Valdez was working the races at Muroc in 1998. He was driving this lacquered bare metal and slammed full custom '50 business coupe; Terry Hunt showed up at Muroc in '98 with his freshly painted "Guam Reality" '53 Studebaker after running it in it's original desert baked paint.

images. The second aspect is the sense of time and place in much of their work, which corresponds with the time/place interests that I have in the hot rod culture. It has a lot to do with the "history" of the hot rod in a visual sense. Hot rods, not street rods, have this timeless sense of place which works in a minimalist landscape. El Mirage, Muroc and Bonneville are beautiful places to photograph this culture and conversely, that is where the culture has its conceptual roots. The relationship of the cars, people and the environment is paramount in the final image. The history is still there, as is the pure sense of hot rodding and what it was, and is, all about. The direct quest of speed and all of the aesthetic and functional modifications made to the car to bring this about. The more work I do photographing the culture, the more I find myself drawn to the land speed racing culture. There is a dignity and a formalistic and spatial visual relationship that lends itself to black & white photography. The images are landscapes, or I should say, cultural landscapes that center on the cars, people and minimalist oriented environment. There are no visual distractions pulling your eye away or confusing the image structure and concept, which is another reason I prefer black & white photography. The salt flats and deserts offer this minimalist setting so conducive to my preference for black & white photography.

If I am photographing a red Deuce out on the salt, and it being seen as red is important, then it's going to dominate the scene (usually) because of the bright color. In a black & white photograph of the same red Deuce, the placement of the Deuce in the surrounding environment brings the viewer directly to the spatial relationship. I'm more interested in the car than the paint and I'm interested in how the car relates to its environment. It's just a hell of a lot easier for me to get this feeling in places like this. There aren't any distractions. The hot rod is con-

ceptually in a time warp, and modern society really crowds and complicates getting an image that I'm satisfied with. Older and rough-edged urban areas also work for me in this way, but it's getting more and more difficult to find and arrange a photographic session with every thing in the right place at the right time.

The foundations and beginnings of the hot rod culture, for many, took place on the dry lake beds of southern California. They were photographed and documented in black & white. Coincidentally, it was at this same period of time, that Ansel Adams & Edward Weston formed the f64 Group of photographers in northern California. This group of very serious and dedicated photographers also favored the medium of straight black & white photography. Both of these events had a profound and lasting effect on my life, but, these two influential forces, through most of my life, have been separate passions. During the Eighties, they began to coincide and finally, in the past decade, really started to join together, focusing on a vision that has taken me back to my roots in photography, as well as my roots with the hot rod and custom culture. The northern California school of straight black & white photography was how I learned the craft, or art, depending on your views, and I still think of absolute photographic reality in black & white terms. The reason I mention all of this is that I seem to be returning to the roots of both cultures, that of hot rods, and that of my foundations in black & white photography. It seems proper, and in a small way, somewhat profound, at least to me. I am satisfying inner urges to bring together both of these passions in my life.

Page 58: Bob Lindstrom's 303-Chrysler-powered D/BGR '32 in front of Russ and Cedric Meeks' hand-formed aluminum '23 T, which is running a 270-inch GMC six.
Page 59: A Bonneville landscape with all of its minimalist simplicity.

Carson TOPS

THE FINAL CHAPTER

Text & Photos By Sherm Porter

Amid the recent resurgence of the custom car craze, we've seen many of the early builders brought out of retirement. Indeed, many, such as Bailon, Emory, Winfield and, of course, Barris, are receiving the accolades they've deserved for being the early pioneers in automotive design. But when it comes to interiors, and custom tops in particular, two names stand out from the rest—Carson and Gaylord.

Carson and Gaylord were both in southern California, and one or the other was responsible for most of all the padded, removable tops being designed and constructed. It was Gaylord who, in the early Fifties, designed a power-driven chopped folding top, and also introduced his version of the popular "California Convertible" top, a cut-down, more modern version, with powerful, rakish lines. But that's another story for another time. We're here to talk Carson.

Now, thanks to a couple of other fine hot rod publications, we already know that Amos "Happy" Carson moved from Salinas, California to Los Angeles in 1927, and he opened the Carson Top Shop on South Vermont Avenue. We also know that Glen Houser went to work for Amos

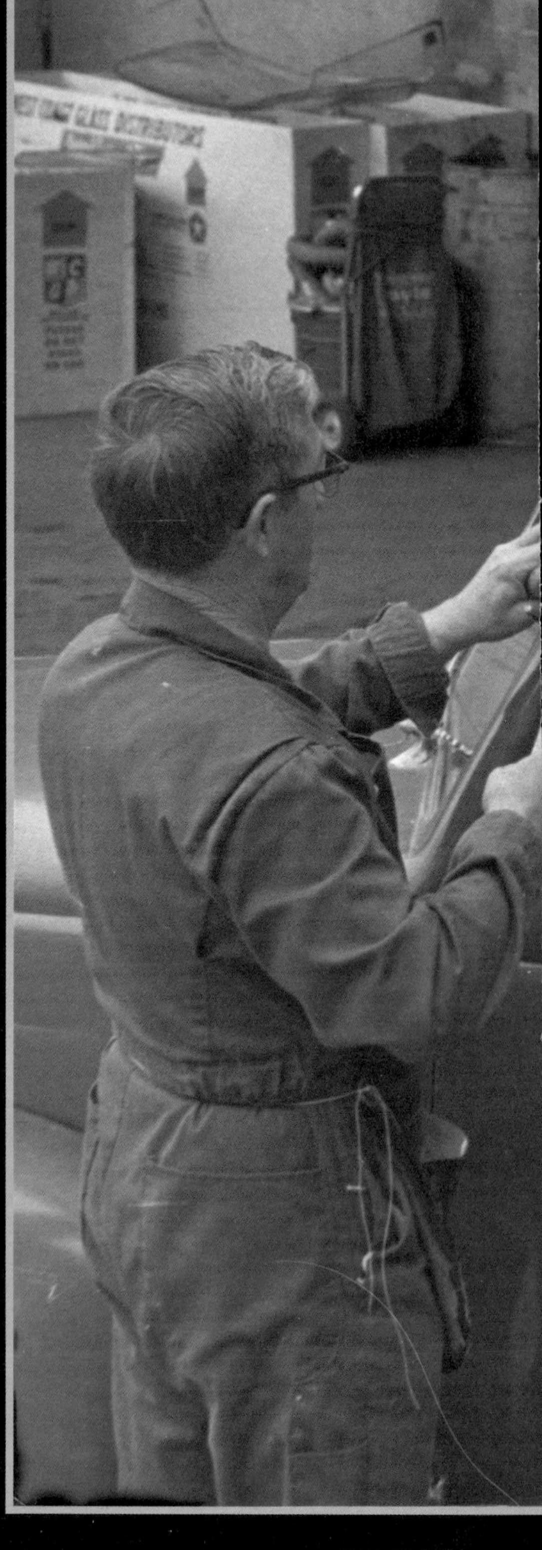

Right: Keith began by removing the old, original padding.; **Inset**: There it is: The original Houser's Carson Padded Tops tag. It's located on the windshield header.

HOUSER'S CARSON PADDED TOPS
PHONE
TH-2308
LOS ANGELES
4910 SO. VERMONT AVE.

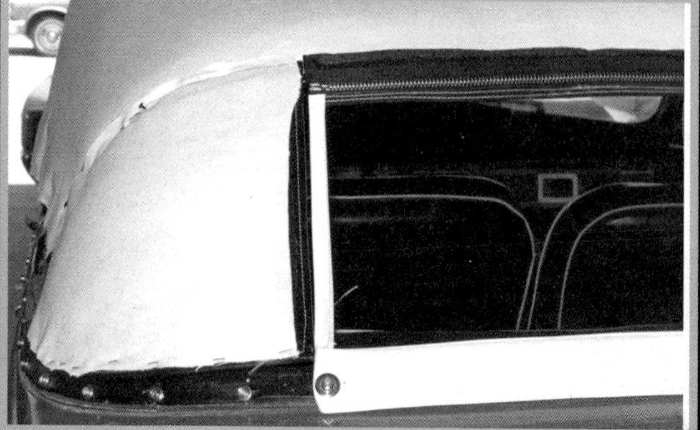

Top to bottom: The original Carson Top framework, stripped and ready to pad. Steel braces are welded along the framework to add strength. Keith inspects all welds, finding no problems; the rear channel is filled to match the bow height. The bows are also padded slightly; here the rear window has been installed, and you can see the undercloth that covers all the fittings.

Opposite page, top to bottom: Keith tacks the webbing in place. You can see the pleated rear quarter panels. A layer of aviary wire keeps the padding from sagging; the final top covering is now installed, beginning with the left side panel; rear window is the plastic "wide" or "open" style; and here we have it, the finished product—the final Carson Padded Top!

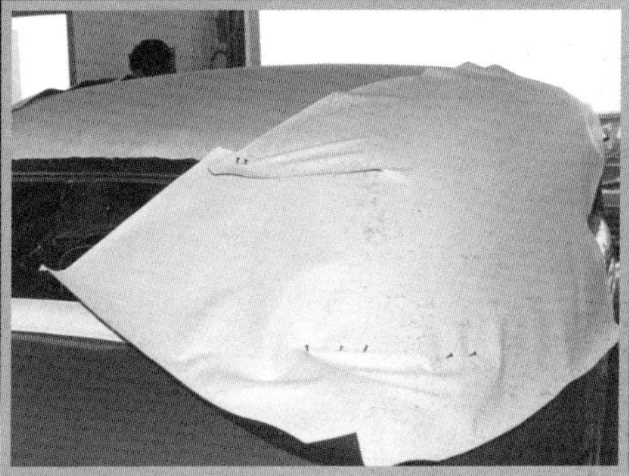

in 1930. Glen immediately set to adding "custom" touches to the tops, and in 1935 designed and built a one-piece, smooth, padded and—of course—non-folding top for a '30 Model A cabriolet. We also know that the shop became very prosperous, and upon his passing in 1942, Amos willed the shop to his employee and close friend, Glen. In 1948, we're told, Glen's son Bob started working at the shop, and they built up the business to the point that, at its peak, was doing 15 tops per week. We also know that, in 1954, the shop moved to a new location on Crenshaw and flourished for a few years, until the custom market started to diminish. The last removable padded top was done in 1965 on a Ford Galaxie show car for George Barris. Glen passed away in 1969, leaving the shop to Bob, who by this time was specializing in vinyl tops for late-model cars. In the mid Seventies Bob retired, closing the shop for the final time, thus ending another chapter in the history of hot roddism.

From the top: The '40, as it looked in 1975; owned for years by Richard Wheeler in West Virginia, the '40 now belongs to Paul Smith of Key Largo, Florida, and is a perfect example of a period custom.

But wait, what we didn't discover was that Bob had another son, Keith. Quietly tucked away in San Luis Obispo, California was Keith's Auto Trim, trimming the local pickups, cars and the occasional airplane seat. And this is where, in 1973, we captured the last Carson Top ever done by a Houser!

The subject vehicle, a '40 Ford convertible, had sat neglected for years in a local battery rebuilder's shop, until a young hot rodder talked him into selling it. After the usual post-storage tinkering—some wiring, gas, air in the tires, and fixing the other normal problems—it was on the street. Then came time to fix it up a bit, which resulted in the meeting with Keith Houser.

A couple of interesting facts on Carson Tops: All material used in making the tops was new, with the exception of the front bow, or header; it was made from the bow of the car for which the top was constructed. The reason for this was simple: The stock bow had shaped itself to the windshield more uniformly than a new bow could. The rear windows were available in three styles and were either glass or plastic. Choices were the standard "small" window, the plastic "wide" opening, and the wraparound or "Coupe de Ville" window. The price depended upon the choice of window and choice of upholstery. The headliners were available in either welted or pipe design, and the plain welting was the best seller. Prices in the early Fifties for a top with the wide window and plain welting were approximately $200 for cars newer than '42; older cars cost a bit less. Jaguar and MG tops (yes, they did sports cars) were $200.

Follow along as we offer you the series of pictures captured in '73, hangin' out at Keith's shop daily, watching (although we didn't know it at the time) another chapter in hot rod history close.

Editor's note: The subject '40 was sold a couple of times in California, with Don Brazil, of Don Brazil Components, being the last West Coast owner. He sold it to Richard Wheeler of West Virginia in 1985, who sold it to yet another "keeper" of history. The car now resides in Key Largo, Florida, with Paul Smith.

RED &
WHITE

Above: Where were you in '56?—Fred was collecting trophies!; **At left**: Fred today—he's not so much the worse for wear either!

THE FRED STEELE Story

50 years of whacked out hot rodding

By Doug Anderson

Get comfortable and grab a cold one, 'cause this is an amazing tale about an unforgettable guy. He's a hot rodder's hot rodder; a guy who not only has the same car passions he started with, but one who still has the same cars!

Fred Steele has been at this roddin' game now for more than 50 years, and he shows no signs of throwing in the towel. Fred tells me he was born at a very early age, in Boston. Times were tough for the young lad, but at 15 he moved out on his own and found a job and a place to sleep at the Jenny gas station in nearby Boxborough. He became friends with the local gear heads who hung out at the station, and many of them had hot cars. The more he rode around with these guys, "racin' and chasin" as he calls it, the more he wanted a rod of his own. Though it was tough on a pump jockey's pay, he began building the Deuce roadster that would become "Purple Pride" in 1951. Little did he know what a path he'd chosen for his life. Many's the night he would prowl downtown Boston in search of chrome, girls, and flathead speed parts—not necessarily in that order. It was during this period that he supplemented his income by selling sombrero hubcaps from late-model Caddys to local customizers—still a hot item in some circles.

After three or four years building the Deuce, doing car shows and moonlight street races, his pride and joy was featured in the July '56 issue of *Rod & Custom*. While building the roadster in the summer of '52, Fred became one of the founding members

From the top: Here she is: "Purple Pride"—started in 1951, winning trophies and appearing in *Rod & Custom* by '56—still fun after 50 years!; here's a formal portrait—they both look purty darn good, 'eh?

of the Boston area Ty-Rods, a rowdy bunch if there ever was one. There's been an incredible trail of projects, adventures, and magazine articles ever since.

I don't believe Fred ever sold a car he's owned, choosing instead to stash them away in the greater Boston area. A veritable "black hole" of hot rodding, Fred has made it tough for the rest of us to find Deuce grille shells. Most of his rides are in prime shape and ready at a moment's notice for a midnight cruise or some such.

Because there are so many cool cars in Fred's varied collection, we'll let the photos tell most of the story. But here are highlights of some of his more memorable:

After finishing the purple Deuce in 1955, the next car he tackled was a '28 A sedan, built in 1957 from the ground up and painted to match the Deuce. For the sedan he chose a 265 Chevy mill, as by that time he could see they were terror on the streets. A '39 Lincoln Zephyr lost its tranny, and it was hooked to a Columbia two-speed rear. The wheels were handmade from A centers cut down and mated to 14- and 15-inch rims. No wheel companies or credit cards back then, boys. You did it yourself or it didn't get done. In the summer of '61 Fred and friend Tommy Dawes drove the car cross-country to Tijuana for a white tuck 'n' roll job, which it still has. The A sedan's a great car, even now, "unrestored" as it is.

Next on Fred's "build list" (after watching one too many "77 Sunset Strip"s on TV) was a cute little '20 T roadster that Fred and Don Spinney built in 1961. Fred bought out Don's interest in the car in '62 and flat towed it all the way to California, where it was photographed overlooking L.A. for a Ventures record album in 1964. While living there, Fred joined the LA Roadsters and remains an associate member to this day.

After returning from California, Fred and Don Spinney again collaborated, this time on a butter yellow full-fendered Deuce roadster, installing a 283 Chev mated to an early Ford driveline. Again, Fred bought out Don in 1966. The car still sits in the same condition, in the same garage, and is ready to hit the road.

In the early 1970s, he found and rescued an orphaned '50 Merc Custom that had had a hard life and proceeded to save it by re-doing the entire car. This is the car alongside the '72 boattail Riviera, his latest, that lost 4 inches of its factory roof pillars in 1993. Fred must like the Merc best though, because that's what we usually see him drivin' lately.

I could go on and on, but you get the idea. He's "got *all* the t-shirts," and there's just no catching up to him. He's had way too much of a head start on all of us so don't even try. But check out the photos and see for yourself how nice his cars are. And if you happen to see a bright yella Merc sneakin' up in your rearview some day, wait and see who it is. It just might be nice guy Fred. Talk with him a while. He's an amazing guy.

From the top: 1992: Von Steal miraculously discovers long lost '40 Ford American Legion staff car in Massachusetts boneyard...; three more of Fred's honeys. The yeller Deuce roadster was finished in 1959 with a 283 Chevy mill, and early Ford driveline; Fred's whacked '50 Merc was reborn like the phoenix from an old custom in 1976.

HOP UP *Magazine's* INTERIOR HOW-TO

Today's basic, bargain basement hot rod has a couple of cliché elements that are either throw-backs to the "day" or just practical no-buck solutions to functional challenges. One of the classics is the saddle blanket, army blanket, serape—there's a hundred of 'em—used to cover a seat spring or whatever it is that keeps your ass off that hot floor.

We figgered that it might be convenient to have an expert trimmer tell us how he would attack the project, share that with us and give us a little insight into—how to.

Swell Tom is a pal. He's done the interior work on some real recognizable hot rods (Flint/Kofoed/Orosco, Spencer/East/Meyer come to mind), but he has more credentials with classics. You know, the Marmons, Mercers, and so on that take something other than production-shop skills to do. He works by himself, fabricates aluminum linings before making seats, frameworks, doors, hatches, spare tire receptacles. He basically makes a deserving science out of a craft that we take for granted.

He took this on anyway!

The issue at hand is an empty tub ('32 Phaeton) that Bellman is about to fire up. He hasn't decided what to do with the seats and kinda needs something to cushion the ride in the buggy spring-suspended early iron. With a short list of hand tools and a reasonably priced shopping list of materials, His Swellness, in a little over two hours, produced the functional, tight, and—Glory

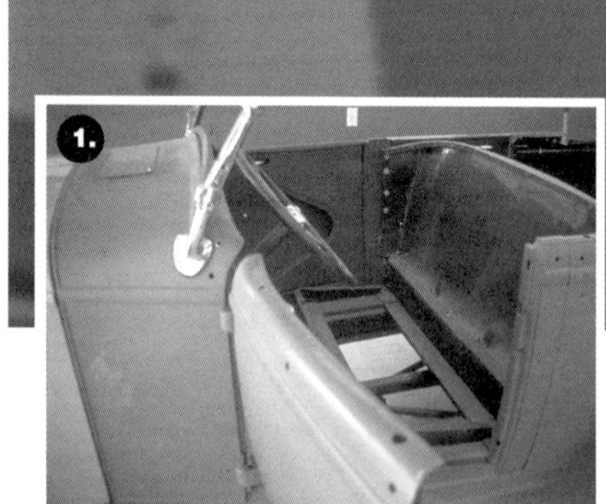

1: Our subject gow job has its original seat riser and other doodads that we'll consider an advantage.

2: Material and tools necessary for the job. It's clear you don't have to go to the machine shop to do this one, eh? **3**: Make cardboard templates for seat bottom and back, noting that there are existing locating pegs for the seat base, and there are retaining clips for the seat back spring that can be employed to brace the plywood material. Contour the patterns if necessary; an irregular shape here is a small price to pay for a seat base/back with appropriate inclination. **4**: Transfer the template pattern to the plywood with whatever you've got. How 'bout a pencil? **5**: Cut the plywood from your scribed pencil markings, sand off splinters and bad edges, and drill alignment holes. You may have to fab some bracketry to attach the two pieces or to align them to your ideal cruising attitude. Make them part of the car, while easily removable for service and when looking for missing church keys, etc.

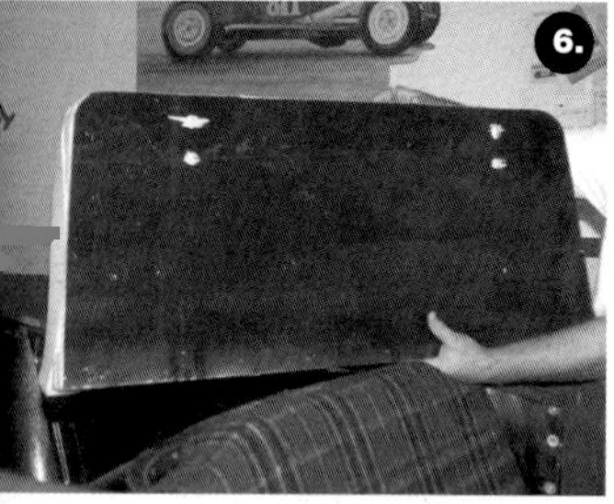

6: Two sets of alignment holes were drilled to facilitate adjustment of the base. Two inches of additional legroom may be what it takes to make the next driver comfortable. **7**: Trial fit the plywood base and back, plop the foam in and sit on it, too.

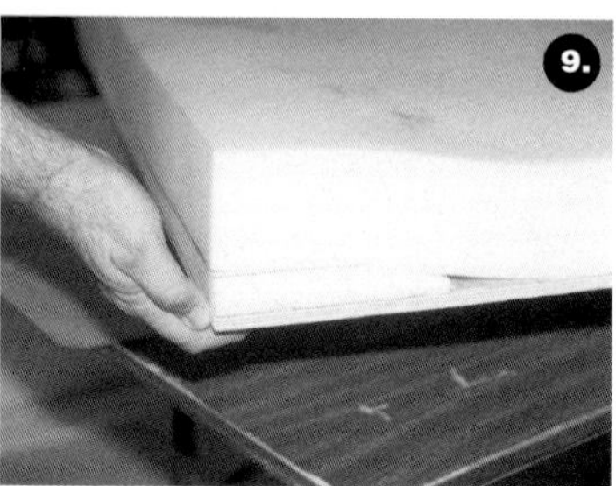

8: Cut the 3-inch foam bottom and back cushions with a hacksaw blade or electric knife, using the plywood for a pattern. Straight cuts will be rewarded later when affixing the "upholstery." **9**: Now cut the 1-inch material to provide the lumbar "kick" and thigh support. This step is crucial in maximizing the seat's function. Use upholstery adhesive to glue the foam pieces. While it's drying, lay out the blankets to schedule patterns, seams, etc., with cushion corners and sides. Misaligned patterns will telegraph apparent carelessness.

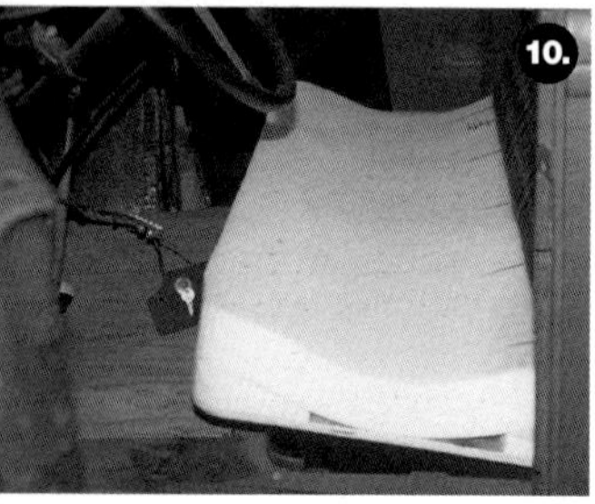

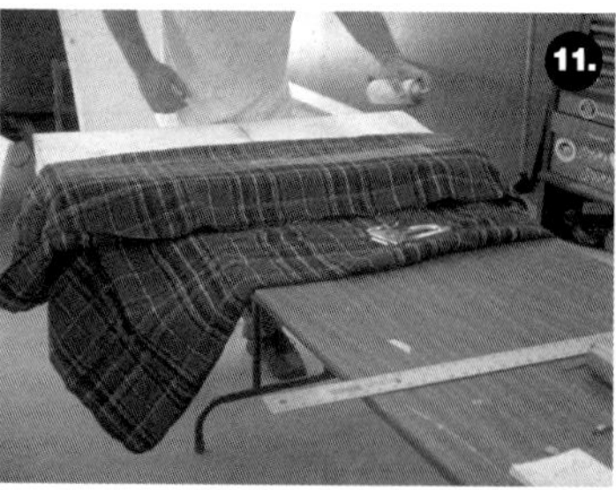

10: Trial fit again. Look for irregular cuts that may confound the blanket attachment, and trim them to suit. **11**: Glue the blanket material to the foam. This is optional, but we thought there would be no later need to separate them, and that the seat would feel more integrated if the field of the material was continuously attached.

12: Staple tightly around the edges, pulling the material taut. Make military-like folds for corners. Sewell makes this look easy...we're not so sure! Trim excess. **13**: Install seat and back. Try it out. Oh, Baby.

Be!—good-looking front seat you see here.

The tools were those that you might find in an average Philistine's garage: jigsaw, staple gun, straight edge, pencil, drill motor and bits, scissors, etc.

The materials accrued to less than $100 and included two pieces of 3-inch foam, two pieces of 1-inch foam, two discarded sheets of 5/8-inch plywood (one for the seat back, one for the seat bottom), upholstery glue, and two new stadium blankets from the local cheapo department store. Foam and glue can be found at upholstery supply houses.

Follow the step by step pictures and captions, make some notes on that empty six pack over there, and soon you'll have a refined surface on which to place that Foxy Mommy-0 of yours when you take her for a ride, hair blowin' all 'round her face with nuthin' but those extra ruby-red lips poochin' out, head tossed back, savoring that balmy 70-mph wind, saying nothing but tossing a look at you when she parts her hair with both hands. And she'll be thinkin,' "Oh, you, you, Hop Up Man, you...."

WHOA DADDY!

Source:

Sewell's Auto Upholstery
Carlsbad, California

HOP UP'S SHOP NITE *FOLLOW-UP*

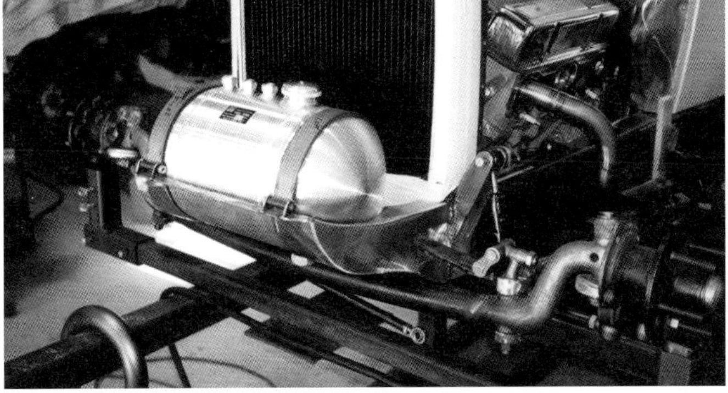

Above from top to bottom: Jim Kitchen's '29 is the long-time street roadster we 'blew apart' last year. It is being morphed into serious race trim for lakes duty this year; Note the handsome fairing Batchelor constructed for Moon Tank cradle. Form and execution exceed race car standards.

From left to right: Frame specifications and hardware applications are products of Batchelor's long experience in this type of fabricating; small block setup will be a Kitchen/Batchelor collaboration. We expect performance will match the quality of the build.

A War Can't Stop A HOT RODDER!

By Albert Drake

Organized hot rodding barely got going in Southern California before WWII shut it down. Muroc dry lake was taken over by the Army Air Force, and soon after gasoline and tires were rationed. A national 35-mph speed limit was imposed. On June 1, 1942, the government decreed that all automobile racing stop, the only sport to be terminated for the duration.

But the same American ingenuity and independence that was helping us win the war was also at work as some boys continued to build cars in the face of adversity. Bob Hammel was one. Before the war, he had been a civilian aircraft mechanic for the Army Air Force. His daily transportation was a neat '30 Ford A-V8 roadster with a genuine DuVall windshield, 21-stud engine with Federal-Mogul heads, Edelbrock slingshot manifold and a plaque that identified him as a member of the Sirocco car club.

When the war began he sold his roadster and joined the Navy. His first posting was Ellyson Field in Pensacola, Florida. Although he was a long way from home, the cars seemed to find him! "Early in my stay...I spotted a sad looking '35 roadster sitting forlornly in front of the BOQ (Bachelor Officer's Quarters). The front end was a disaster and it was very pigeon-toed, having had an encounter with a cow."

Bob found the officer who owned the car and was able to buy it for $50 down and $50 when he got the title. Because he had "night check" duty he was able to work on the Ford during the day. The first task was to find the necessary parts.

"At that time in Pensacola, the junk yards were full of choice parts for little money," Bob recalled. "I found a complete '36 [Ford] front end, including the radiator, which started my task of converting the '35 into a '36. I fitted '34 Pontiac hood sides, '40 Oldsmobile bumpers, '39 Lincoln Zephyr taillights, Zephyr wheel discs, Buick skirts—all the usual Los Angeles 'custom parts.'" Although the rear fenders were in good shape, Bob replaced them with '36 rear fenders to make the conversion complete

The black "Hollywood" custom created quite a stir on the streets of Pensacola, where modified cars were extremely rare. Service station attendants were startled when they raised the hood and saw the dual carb set-up. Bob made the two-carburetor intake manifold in the manner of the Jack Henry manifolds he had seen. He got an early '32 Ford single-throat manifold, welded up the carburetor flange, and then fabricated a platform and down tubes on which he mounted a pair of Stromberg 97s with chromed short stacks. The engine also had milled heads and dual pipes with homemade "Smitty" mufflers.

"I had never received the title from the original owner (who had been shipped out). So I went down to the Florida Motor Vehicle Department and told them that the fellow I had bought the car from was 'missing in action.' They gave me a new title and I registered the car, got insurance, and used the car until I was shipped out.

"Before I shipped out I sold the car to my friend for something down, and he could send me the rest when he had it. I would then send him the title. Needless to say, the balance of the payments never came, but I wasn't worried because I still had the title.

"The only thing I had forgotten was the fact that my friend had gone with me when I was getting my title. So *he* went to the DMV, declared me 'missing in action,' and got a new title!"

Bob was sent to Barber's Point Naval Air Station in Oahu, Hawaii, and he immediately began to build another hot rod. As he recalled, "When they built that air station at

Opposite page, from the top: Bob Hammell and the finished car. Note the "blacked out" headlights required during wartime; Bob Hammel (right) and his buddies resting on the '35 roadster. Note the 1940 Oldsmobile bumper—once a popular item—and the extra lights the previous owner had installed.

From the top: A swell car for a sailor on leave! Skirts are from a Buick. Car was now painted black; Later Bob put 1937 DeSoto bumpers on the car front and back. Those are Lincoln Zephyr taillights; The Chev 4 roadster Bob and his buddies built using a Model T coupe body. Note Whippet radiator shell and Woodlight lamps.

the start of the war, they just bulldozed all the old cars on the property into a pile. As my unit contained quite a number of hot rod guys, we began to search through that pile and came up with a fairly decent '25 four-cylinder Chevy. We chiseled the sedan body off and dragged the chassis and other parts into a little clearing where it wouldn't be seen."

Then they made friends with a junkyard owner in downtown Honolulu. They found a straight 1926 Model T coupe body and cut off the top to make it into a roadster. The doors were cut down, a styling touch that reflects the influence of the pre-war MG and other cars. The 18-inch wire wheels came from a Durant; the grille shell and radiator came from a Whippet 4. Those really neat headlights are called Woods lights; they were used on various luxury cars such as the Ruxton and DuPont. The boys made their own Hallock-type windshield, which looks right at home on this bug. It seems amazing, but they were able to find an Oldsmobile three-port head to put on the Chev block, and they welded up their own Swann-type dual intake manifold.

"It turned out very nice," Bob said of this car built by committee, in a clearing in the bush, during a war. That seems an understatement; that car, like the 1935/36 roadster he built earlier, would attract a crowd of admirers at a rod run today.

Custom Truck Caravan

By Thom Taylor

The only form of customizing today that has a direct link to the customs of the '50s are the lowered late-model Chevy and Ford "sport trucks" most prevalent in California. "No way," you say? Then read on.

Customizing was a way to modernize and individualize a car or truck. Customizers tried to stay up with, or in some cases lead, what was pouring out of Detroit and even Europe. Today, you don't see late model cars customized—unless you classify the PT Cruiser as a car. The Mercs and shoebox Fords prowling the Greaser events don't count either, as they are throwbacks to the style of customizing done nearly 50 years ago. And though these later custom trucks are homogenized by nature, with their fiberglass off-the-shelf rolled pans, bumper masks and tonneau covers, they are executed in a contemporary vein. Just as their predecessors were contemporary for their time—the '50s.

There were probably more custom haulers roaming the A&W's than chopped Mercs, though they get less mention today. Even George Barris did his fair share of customized trucks, including the radical Kopper Kart, Wild Kat F-100, and parts of the *Rod & Custom* Dream Truck. And all-around custom legend Bill Gaylord had a succession of custom pickups that served double duty as shop trucks and weekend haulers for his first love: ski boats.

So a tribute to the custom truck is in order. Besides, I needed to do something with these single images of trucks found in the James Potter photo collection. Though not comprehensive, these random shots will give you an idea of the variety of types and styles of customized pickups found roaming both the northern and southern California suburbs in the later half of the '50s.

Hopefully these photos will stimulate you to consider a truck for your next project. They're still relatively cheap, easy to find parts for, and functional, besides. And with less glass, trim and seats than a comparable sedan, they are probably less costly to customize.

Thanks to Greg Sharp for some of the information provided.

Top: The Omaha, Nebraska crew for Norm Coborg's Golden Rod '34 coupe drew quite a lot of attention, stemming partially from their cool '56 Mercury tow truck. Converted fire salvage sedan was the work of Larry Fritsch, who also painted the coupe. Gold and black "Ranchero" was created using 2-inch tubing for the hand-made bed, and '41 Ford hood for the rear of the top. Shot is from 1957. **Left to right:** Close-up shot of Ed Roth's flamed shop truck in '58. The blends in the flames were still being done by layering the paint and then sanding through to the underlying colors. Rake, paint, Olds spinners, chrome running boards and spots were the extent of the customizing found on "Big Daddy's" hauler; interim shot of Spence Murray's *Rod & Custom* Dream Truck before fins and final paint. Custom front end is in its final form, but the rear of the truck has yet to see the torch. Primer scallops are different than the final painted version. Construction ran from '54 to '58.

From the top: Babe's Muffler '50 Ford pickup from San Jose, California, was fairly radical for a "shop truck." Babe Royer's work included the chopped top, Nash grille, '53 Ford headlight rings; George Mitobe's Watson-flamed Ranchero featured many custom touches including mesh grille, rolled rear pan with hand-made nerfs, and Edsel wagon tail lights; compare Mitobe's Ranchero to Renegades-member Bill Moore's "Sugar Plum." Many similar touches throughout, with Moore's retaining the rear bumper.

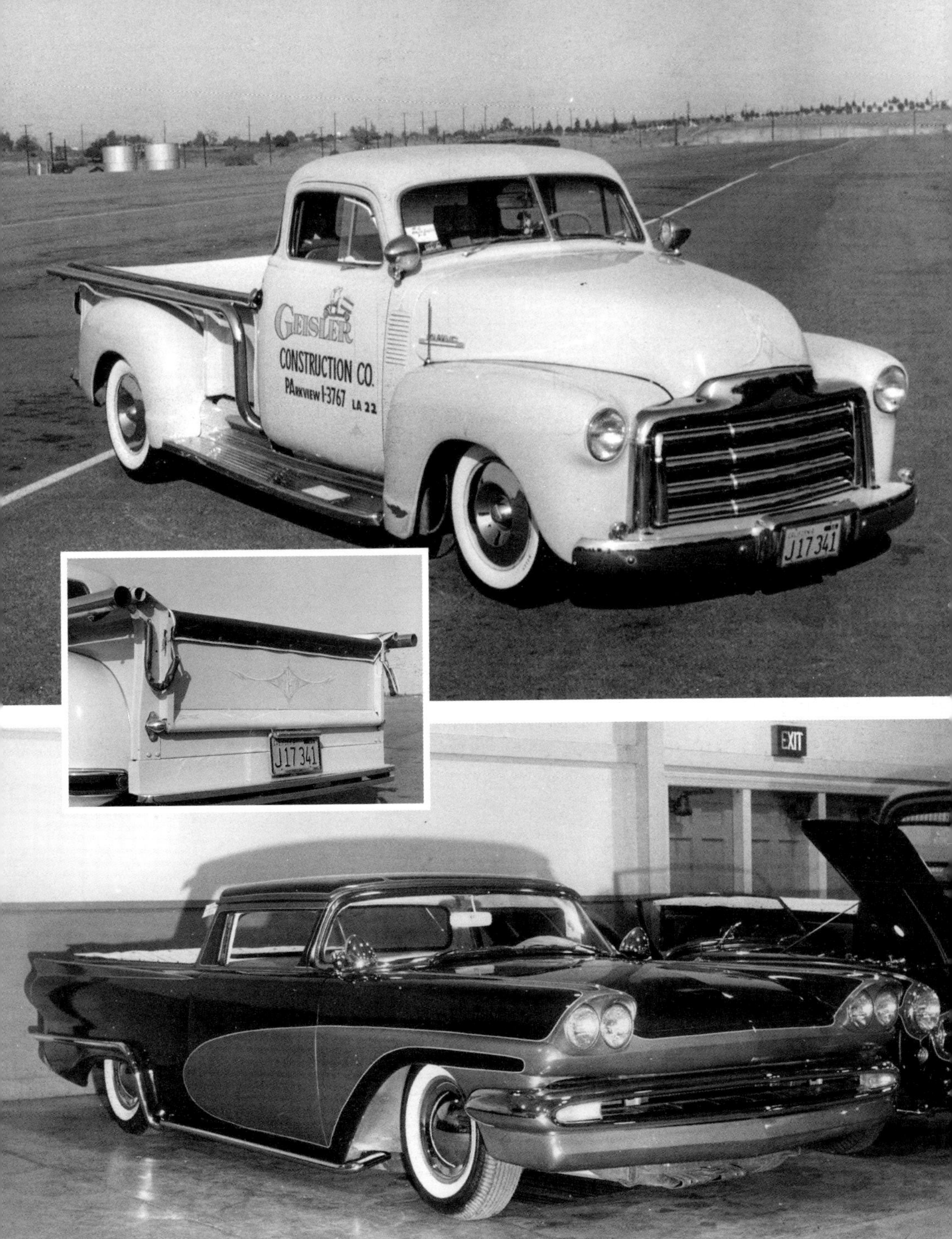

From the top: Bruce Geisler's chopped GMC looks very much today like it did in this 1957 Potter photo. Though rarely seen in custom pickups today, exhaust exiting along the bed was way cool in the 50's; rear detail of Geisler's Jimmy shows Merc taillights, custom bumper, tonneau, smoothed tailgate, extension below the bed and bed rail exhaust; this highly customized '58 Ranchero led a double life on the show car circuit. Its first incarnation is seen here in late '58, owned by Dick Tiago. Features included a 3-inch chop with green and lime paneling by Ward's in Alameda, California. Rolled front pan incorporated a '57 Desoto bumper. After a bad wreck the Ford was restyled and billed as the "outer space-styled custom" built by Bill Ortiz.

The Story Of

TWIN CITIES AUTOMOTIVE

Text & Photos by Aaron Kahan

Back in the summer of 1992, my friend Jim Aust called and asked if Jon "Fish" Fisher and I wanted to go look at a '29 roadster on Deuce rails that he was interested in trading for his cabriolet project. Jim was one of the first young hot rodders I met besides my close club buddies. We were both in our early twenties and owned '32 Fords. I had had my five-window for a couple of years, and Jim was building a Forties-style flathead-powered Deuce cabriolet.

It turned out that the '29 roadster was located in the Sunland/Tujunga area of Southern California. When we arrived at Sam Lirones' place he was not home, and after waiting a while it was apparent that he had forgotten our meeting. The gate was open so we let ourselves in, and before our eyes was a backyard scattered with cars covered in blue tarps.

As we began to uncover the cars we discovered there was way more than just a '29 roadster on Deuce rails resting in Sam's backyard. In fact, there was a jaw-dropping assortment of hot rods that were obviously built before the mid-Sixties. Besides a lot of miscellaneous speed equipment and early hot rod parts, there were six complete hot rods for sale. The '29 roadster was the first one we looked at. It was wearing old black paint, sitting on Deuce rails, and featured a chromed early Halibrand rearend, Auburn dash, and a Deuce grille shell. Next to it sat a full fendered '29 roadster pickup running an early Chevy V8 and a faded orange paint job. In front of the garage was a channeled '27 T roadster with an early Cadillac motor, roll bar, and full disc covered 16-inch wheels.

We couldn't get inside the garage, but hiding behind the door were tons of parts and a super bitchin' chopped '39 Ford convertible. It sat hot rod style with a louvered hood, folding top, and a flathead motor. On the other side of the garage was another full fendered '29 roadster pickup wearing faded old yellow paint, a '27 T bed, dropped headlight bar, and steel wheels. The final car of the bunch was an odd hot rod.

Top:: Overview of Sam Lirones' backyard shows Nick's old '27 T roadster by the garage. The two other cars eventually became Choppers club hot rods; **Left to right:** Jon "Fish" Fisher's '29 A-V8 looked like this when he dragged it home. With much help from Lynn "Swifty" Bird the Deuce frame and running gear were completely reworked into a late Forties/early Fifties-style hot rod; Nick had set up the '27 T roadster ready to race with a Cad motor, roll bar, sprint car steering wheel and a full belly pan.

From the top: This was the other running car Nick had. The yellow '29 roadster pickup features a '27 T bed, dropped headlight bar, shortened Deuce grille shell, lowered stance and steel wheels. The one in front of it was definitely Nick's oddest rod. It looks to be a shortened Model A four-door sedan sitting on a Deuce frame with a suicide mounted front end. I wonder if anybody out there has finished this project?; Choppers member Jon "Fish" Fisher and girlfriend Julie motor towards Paso Robles in May of '97, a little over a year after he got his A-V8 on the road. The roadster still wears the same black paint and blue painted grille shell that it had when he took it home; Dave Defever rebuilt Nick's old roadster into this configuration and then sold the almost running bitchin' hot rod at the '93 L.A. Roadster Show.

It appeared to be a shortened four-door Model A sedan, turned into a two-door, sitting on Deuce rails with a suicide front end.

By now, all I could think of was where did all these hot rods come from, and did any of them have documented history? I was just dying to know the story of these hot rods. We eventually left Sam's house with tons of questions but no answers.

A couple of days later I got the scoop from Jim. Sam had recently bought this bunch of rods from Nick Nicholson. Many people had tried to buy Nick's hot rods, but he would never agree on a price. Nick also decided that he would only sell his cars as a collection and not individually. Somehow Sam managed to sum up a deal to purchase all of Nick's hot rods, parts, and cool speed equipment, for about $30,000. When Sam purchased this mother load, all the rods were stored in makeshift garages at Nick's mom's house in Tujunga. Sam's plan was to keep the chopped '39 convertible and sell the other cars and parts to finance its rebuild.

I don't know what happened to all the cars, but Sam decided he didn't want to trade Jim for his cabriolet, and Fish ended up buying the '29 roadster. The orange '29 roadster pickup was parted out, and Burbank Tire's Jim Martin ended up with the body and fenders. He built the truck and got it running with a flathead motor, and it eventually ended up in Verne Hammond's garage. The channeled '27 T roadster was bought by Dave Defever, who got the car about 90-percent done and then sold it to current owner Mike Hight. Last I heard, Sam was modernizing his '39 by taking off all the cool parts, like the old louvered hood, and making chassis updates that included installing a Jaguar rearend.

I wanted to find out some more about Nick Nicholson, so I called my friends Frank Guildner and John Williamson, who live in Sunland. They told me that Nick ran a hot rod shop in Tujunga called Twin City Automotive from the late Forties to the early Sixties. Nick's shop was painted black and so was his belly-panned roadster. Most of Nick's hot rods were never drivers, just continuous projects or cars built for display. The Cad-powered T and the yellow roadster pickup were drivers and were regularly spotted on the road. Nick's hot rods were at various Autorama shows back in the old days.

Besides being a car builder, Nick was an eccentric writer type who wrote for various car mags in the Fifties. He also owned a chopped '34 Ford three-window lakes racer and a Deuce roadster. George Williams was able to buy Nick's channeled Deuce roadster before Sam's big purchase, and was the only person able to purchase one of Nick's cars individually. In the Seventies Nick moved his shop to Hollywood into what eventually became Dean Jeffries' current digs. After all the years of building and collecting, Nick eventually moved all his stuff to his mom's house in Tujunga when he inherited it in the late Seventies. Everything remained there until the day Sam hauled it all to his home, just a short distance away from Twin City Automotive's original location.

Unfortunately, Nick passed away a couple years back and the name "Twin City Automotive" has vanished from the modern hot rod world. Nick Nicholson would be happy to know that a majority of his old rods are back on the road where they belong!

From the top: Nick's old roadster today. Most of the parts Nick originally used are still on the car. Current owner Mike Hight got this rod back on the road where it belongs; Verne Hammond's '29 roadster pickup was acquired from Burbank Tire's Jim Martin in '99. Since purchasing the hot rod pickup, Verne has channeled the body, removed the fenders, added an Auburn dash, mocked it up with Kelsey Hayes rims, and will possibly use the nerf bars that came with the truck; back in '93 a guy named Richard bought the Cadillac headers that were once on Nick's '27 T roadster (and were originally on Norm Grabowski's Kookie Car) from Dave Defever at the L.A. Roadster Show. A few months ago, Deacon's member John Bade responded to an ad in the recycler for some Auburn panels and ended up buying the headers from Richard for a mere $75. Not a bad deal for a serious piece of hot rod history.

COLOR M

KANSAS CITY

GONE!

All photographs copyright Julian Silverberg
By Ron Thums

Ask most of us here in 2001 to describe the early years of drag racing and we likely conjure up mental images of 1964-era front-motored fuelers like the Prudhomme-Black and Ivo cars—iconic vehicles whose colorful livery has been burned into that part of our car-guy memory that catalogs these things. Now, we know there were dragsters earlier on, but they must've been kinda tiny, colorless things, because that's the way we've always seen them in those 40-year-old hot rod mags. Imagine my surprise a couple years ago to discover that my own father-in-law had tucked away a handful of rolls of color slides from drag racing's early days in a shoebox. An amateur photographer and long-time car nut, his thing has always been the wire wheel set, with subjects tilting toward skinny-tired MGs, Triumphs and Alfas on the winding road courses of Elkhart Lake and other Midwestern tracks. But a visit to California in 1952 found him at the Los Angeles Fairgrounds in Pomona; and he turned up at the "Olympics of Drag Racing" in Kansas City, Missouri, on Labor Day weekend in 1956.

KANSAS CITY
Top: This beautiful Deuce roadster was cleaner than most. **From the left**: Bob Alsenz shoed Kenny Lindley's beautiful blown Chrysler-powered "Miss Fire II" to top speed of the meet at 159.01 mph. The Anaheim, California, team took home the "Best Engineered" award: a new Chrysler Hemi and a 55-gallon drum of nitro for their effort; The B/Open Gas "Flying Wedge" was sponsored by Suburban Automotive in Cicero, Illinois; Keith Bain of Dumas, Texas won a new engine for turning 115 mph in his '56 Plymouth-pushed B/Open Gas rail.

KANSAS CITY
Above: Ed Cortopassi of Sacramento, California, wheeled the beautiful plastic-bodied "Glass Slipper" to top Chev-powered speed of the weekend: 141.50 mph with an e.t. of 10.57. The since-restored Cortopassi & Davis car lost in eliminations on the final day-after swapping in a flathead Merc(!)

KANSAS CITY
Above: 30-year-old Art Arfons became the first member of *Hot Rod* magazine's "150 mph Club," turning that number out of the gate on opening day. The Akron, Ohio, feed-grain business operator's "Green Monster #6" A/Dragster was powered by a 1710-cube, 1450-hp V-12 Allison aircraft engine. **At right:** Otie Smith of Akron, Ohio, turned 115 mph in his 265-cube Chev-powered '27 T roadster.

KANSAS CITY
Left: Bob Rodgers of Muncie, Kansas, turned top Oldsmobile-powered time of the meet (131.77 mph) in his bellytank and won a new Olds engine. **Right**: The "Quad-Cities Ignitors" club plate places this sano rear-engine car as being from the Davenport, Iowa/Moline, Illinois area. Gotta love the Thickstun marine splash covers on the flathead motor.

POMONA
Above: We think this may be Chuck Price's '32 roadster, which was the first *Rod & Custom* cover car. **Left:** This little slingshot digger is the first of a long string of "Bean Bandits" cars driven by the legendary Joaquin Arnett of San Diego, California.

POMONA
Right: The Cad convert and Chevy with Olds grille look out of place among the dedicated racecars at the '52 drags. We wonder if Cadillac racer Tommy Baker had anything to to do with the Caddy?

POMONA
Left: We don't have any information on this '36 5-window. It looks to be a precursor of a Sixties gasser, doesn't it?

POMONA
Above: Safety equipment was, shall we say, rudimentary at the digs in '52? Note that there's no fence to protect the spectators, either. Left: Check out the rather scary seat frame and steering on "The Flea." The rollbar's a little strange, too, but they tried. At least it looks like those hefty framerails would survive a rollover intact. Very cool push car, though.

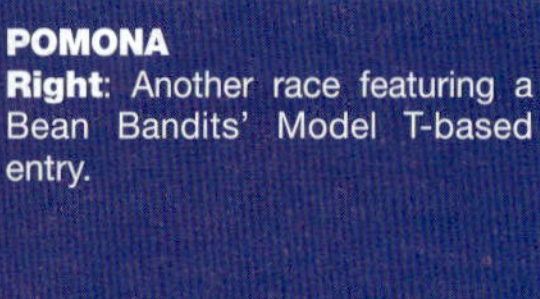

POMONA
Right: Another race featuring a Bean Bandits' Model T-based entry.

POMONA
Left: Another view of Bean Bandit Joaquin Arnett's digger. With a 275-inch Merc running 50 to 80 percent nitro, the squirrelly (84-inch wheelbase) 1,325-pound car set track records throughout the state in '52-'53, reaching speeds of 134 mph.

POMONA
Above: Looks like the Model A got the hole-shot on the Deuce, at least past the timing tower. **Left**: The striped nose marks this as Ak Miller's modified roadster, which turned 160 mph at El Mirage.

POMONA
Right: Now *this* is a race team stripped to the basics: No body on the car, no push vehicle, just a lot of guts and muscle. Definitely Hop Up Guys.

POMONA
Left: The staging area in 1952. Visit the Winternationals in Pomona today and it's hard to believe it's the same place. Only the phone poles haven't changed much.

The Golden Anniversary

This is for the gold—*Hop Up*'s Fiftieth Anniversary. In this commemorative issue, we have tracked down a handful of the cars (and people) that appeared in the first couple of years of *Hop Up*—while it was still a little book—and present them here in cameo form.

It's notable that the cars of *Hop Up* have been preserved at maybe a higher rate than others, a testament to their timeless aesthetics and to the apparent selectivity of the editors at the time. Yes, there was what we have heard called a "West Coast bias," but we rather think that that was where the office, finances, staff and cameras were. There certainly was enough local talent to report on, and there was no politically correct mandate to offer nationwide equity in rod reporting, although they aspired to it without regional jealousy.

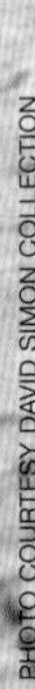
PHOTO COURTESY DAVID SIMON COLLECTION

Other geographic areas were not forsaken because of territorial snobbishness. Instead, there probably just wasn't the budget to chase cross-country in a search for subjects to fill a few pages when there was ample fodder for the success of the mission right in their own backyard. And dry lake. Resistance to freelance submissions might have been a product of, "Pay him, or pay me?" realities. We don't know.

What we do know is that we have been able to compile the following chapter, including some feature-size articles, that tell us where the *Hop Up* features of "the day" are… today.

Fifty frickin' years. Think about it.

THE GOLDEN ANNIVERSARY

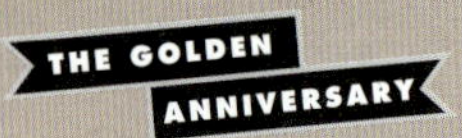

Barney NAVARRO

BENCH RACING WITH A LEGEND

By Ken Gross

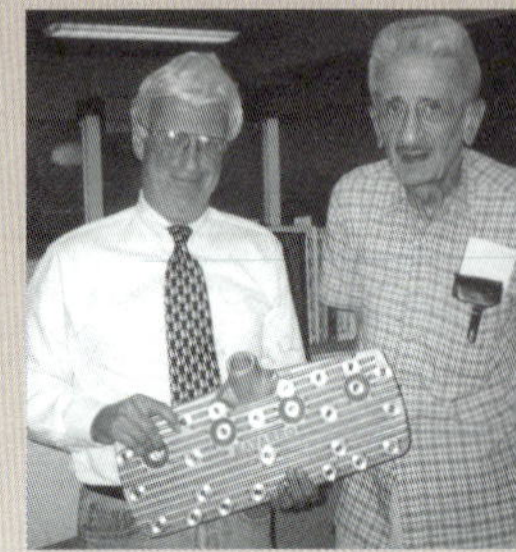

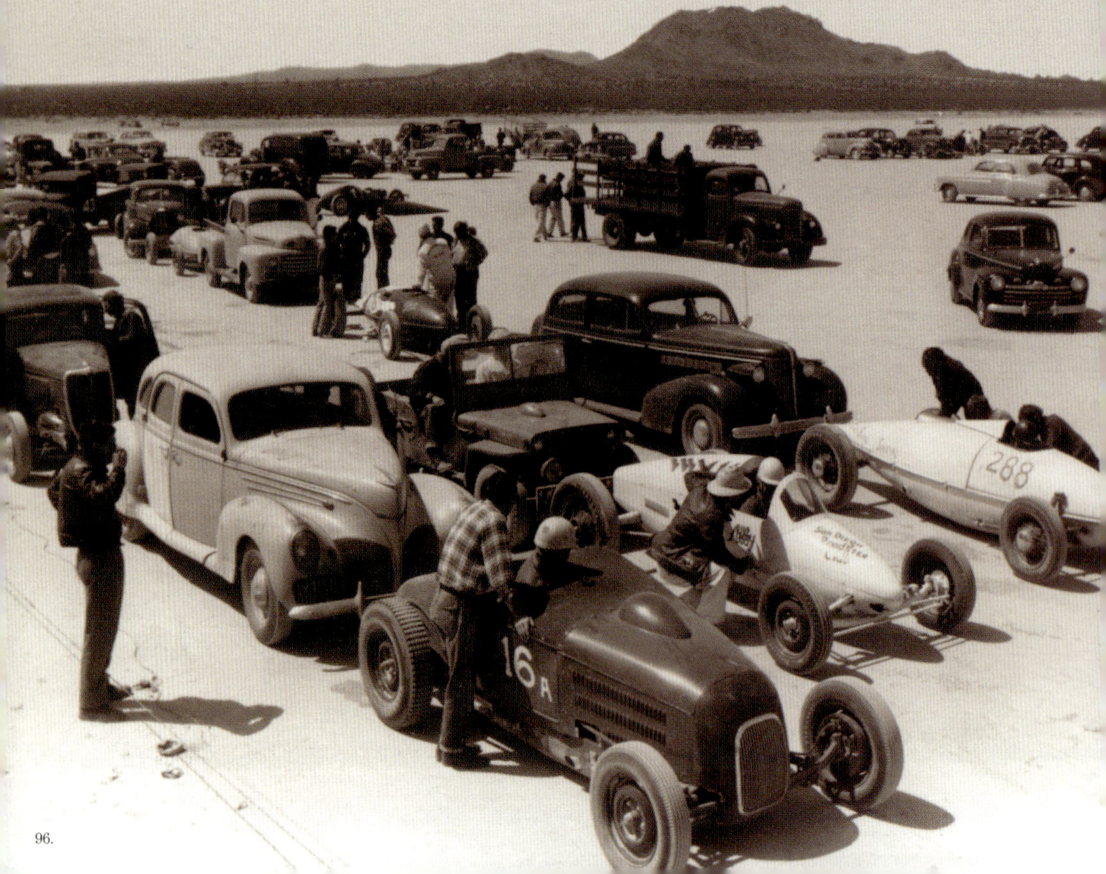

Barney Navarro, an authentic dry lakes hero, holds court in a cluttered office in his small machine shop in East Los Angeles. He's been here for three decades and it shows. Vintage milling machines and drill presses share the crowded space with a computerized mill. In one corner, stacks of unfinished three-carburetor Navarro intakes await final machining. Freshly minted finned alloy Navarro high-compression heads, still considered among the best for the Ford flathead, are piled on old wooden shelves.

The machine shop is clean and neat, if a bit dark by contemporary standards. Everywhere you glance, there's a leaden patina you could get only after 32 years of hard use. It's like a time warp. Close your eyes and you can hear the din of machinery and imagine a dozen sweating men toiling away amidst oil and swarf.

Open your eyes and it's very quiet. Eighty-year-old Barney is suffering from the mobility ills that plague the aging, but his fertile mind has lost none of its sharpness.

A hot rodder since the late Thirties, Barney's always possessed an eclectic blend of practical and theoretical wisdom. An expert machinist and mechanic, he was featured in the very first issue of *Hop Up*, back in July, 1951, in a five-page article by Lou Kimzey called "To the Lakes with Barney." Kimzey described how in just 39 nonstop hours, including the time it took him to drive to El Mirage, the indefatigable Navarro bought a brand new flathead block, ported and relieved it, fitted a destroked 180-degree crank of his own making and installed it in his Class A roadster.

That day, Navarro ran 109 mph with a 182-cid engine he hadn't even fired until he got to the lakes and was clocking about 135 on alcohol (by his tach) when the fuel backfired through the oxygen-injected twin carbs and his engine caught fire. The final photo shows Navarro putting out the blaze himself with a Pyrene extinguisher.

Barney authored many articles himself in *Hop Up*, and later did the same in *Hot Rod*,

always focusing on why things worked the way they did. Here's a bit from a story he wrote in March, 1952, entitled, "How Many Pots?" It's vintage Navarro: "If one more helps, a lot should do wonders. This is the line of reasoning that is often applied to carburetion. After installing a basket of carburetors, the budding mechanic expects his car to leap like a jackrabbit when he punches the throttle. However, such a procedure often causes bitter disappointment rather than the fabulous performance that's expected. In fact, it is actually possible (and he goes on to explain why) to add so much carburetion to an engine that the car will slow down if the engine is floored under 35-mph in top gear...." Good advice, 48 years ago and now.

Barney Navarro clearly understood the principles of mechanics, chemistry and physics that made engines work. His record-breaking efforts and his own speed equipment reflected what he believed. As Tom Sparks, himself a talented mechanic, recently told me, "Barney was a thinker. He didn't just follow people. He did what *he* thought was right. His equipment worked. That's why I used it."

Barney's hot rodding career started with a Hudson six. "It was all I could afford, initially," he says with a chuckle. "Besides, the Ford V8 to me was sort of a misbegotten engine. I was critical of them when I was a kid because most of the Fords overheated. Due to the exhaust going through the block, the back end of the block would get red hot. Because of that, (Henry) Ford couldn't use nickel iron; he had to use soft iron or the expansion difference would cause it to break up into many pieces. But a friend of a friend had a new '35 Ford, and he drove it like a madman. He'd forget sometimes it was in second gear. He'd be doing 70 miles an hour, wondering why it wasn't going faster. I thought, despite the Ford's shortcomings, it had a certain resistance to destruction I didn't see in other cars."

As a collector of vintage Ford speed equipment myself, I had to ask Barney why there were so many different manifold, ignition and camshaft designs. "Following a sheep won't give you success," he says. "You have to go down a different path than the rest. And when you do that, you've got to learn what the rest of them don't know."

Barney always preferred smaller displacement engines, destroked cranks, and pop-up pistons. His path to power was admittedly different from the guys who piled on carburetors and stroked the daylights out of their engines. "It's what the rule book would allow," he says. "They proscribe what you can do, so you do like a lawyer would. You ask, where are the loopholes? Where do I change from what we had? You have to think about this as a lesson in physics. Think about Newton's first law of motion-for every action, there's an equal and opposite reaction."

Before the war, he bought a '39 Ford Tudor and joined the Glendale Stokers, a club that included rodding luminaries like Doane Spencer. "You had to belong to a club to go to the dry lakes."

Barney was working in the Heydrich Brothers' machine shop down in Los Angeles, making equipment for aircraft companies that required intricate die work. "That helped me quite a bit in spatial visualization. They let me rent the shop on weekends to make things on my own. At Heydrich's one weekend, I took the stock cast iron heads off my flathead. I didn't like the big turbulence cavity they had; it lowered the compression considerably. So I milled these heads about 1/8th of an inch, then made a high speed steel doming cutter (which he still has) so I could redome the head, reshape and flycut the combustion chamber. Then someone in the club told me Phil Weiand was getting ready to make intake manifolds. When he got some castings, I machined 10 for him and got one in return.

"In 1941, I was running that Weiand intake

BATCHELOR ARCHIVES/RON KELLOG COLLECTION

BATCHELOR ARCHIVES/RON KELLOG COLLECTION

on my '39. We'd been going out to the outlying country, like Foothill Boulevard, for drag races. I know people turn up their noses at that, but most of us were very safety-conscious. We picked places where there were no crossroads, and we had enough deceleration and braking distance to stop. I put the engine from my Ford in Bud Swanson's modified that November and went to Muroc with it.

"I got to make only one run. There were so many cars, that's all you could do. I got up to 107 mph, grouped with people up to 110. I don't know how many cars lined up; it looked to me as though there were at least 10 of them, and we had this drag race. They dropped the flag and you took off. I was sitting there hoping every one of the guys knew what he was doing, because you couldn't see where you were going with all that dust. What we did on city streets (he laughs) was far safer than that particular event."

Following WWII, and before he was discharged, he designed his own manifold, loosely based on the one on his '42 Ford, a car he'd bought seven days before Pearl Harbor. His first dual manifold, a low-rise affair with a dog-bone shaped removable heat riser, was a result of an experience he'd had crossing the mountains in New Mexico in Winter using the tall, high-rise, pre-war

Weiand manifold. Both carburetors had iced up, and his car slowed to 35 miles per hour, slowly strangling.

Barney decided to improve on that design. "Remember," he says, "the firing order on a flathead alters from bank to bank, except for numbers one and two cylinders which fire sequentially. Every time it fires you have exhaust on one side or the other, so (my design) kept the carburetors warm. For summer use, you simply took out the long center stud and replaced the dog-bone with a little cover." Unfortunately for Barney, it wasn't very popular (though it's a $500-plus collector's item today if you're lucky enough to find one). "People thought an absolutely cold charge gave maximum horsepower; later I built a manifold with the heat riser underneath."

I had to ask Barney about Tom Beatty, who held many records with his Navarro-equipped flathead-powered belly tank. "Tom was one of my employees," Barney recalls. "That's where he learned machine shop practice." He was notorious for blowing up engines, I say. "Yes," says Barney, resignedly, "and it's sad that's what he became notorious for, because there's really no reason to blow up a whole sequence of engines for a week. He used to do a lot of things that you can't get away with—too much boost and not enough strength in the connecting rods, for example.

"The Ford connecting rod is a marvel. It's amazing that it lasts as long as it does," insists Barney. "Believe it or not, that rod is a casting. The bolts are cast integral with the shoulder of the rod. They never revealed what that alloy was. When I built my own engine, I had a small (stock) 3 1/16 bore and used the big Mercury rods. This was to conform to the rules. I felt that the blower gave you enough advantage despite a small 183-ci displacement because you could pump twice as much air into the engine, which means twice the horsepower. I could rev to 8000 rpm (!) with my 180-degree crank without worrying about it."

Barney says he always preferred Ed Winfield's camshafts, particularly a special version of Ed's famed Super 1A grind. Navarro made his own large diameter lifters and cam blanks. I asked him if Winfield was really the genius he was cracked up to be. "He was," says Barney, without hesitation, "but there were some things... (he stops, then continues) ...he didn't quite fully understand. He gave out some information that Clay Smith and Danny Jones, who were partners, were highly critical of, and I agree.

"Ed's trouble," says Navarro, "was that before he had a dyno to test Lou Fageol's engine, every bit of testing was [limited to what they could do] on the road. In the 1920s and '30s, they used the old River Road, which they now call Forest Lawn Drive. You can negotiate a good portion of that road at over 100 miles an hour. They'd drop a racecar off at the end, over near Barham Boulevard and drive their truck to the other end. Then the racer would make a pass through there to see how things worked. Or they'd go someplace out in the San Fernando Valley, which was all farmland then. I used to be able to drive 80 miles an hour down Devonshire."

Barney Navarro was one of many dry lakes rodders, like Vic Edelbrock, Sr., Ed Iskenderian, Charles "Kong" Jackson, Phil Weiand, the Spaulding brothers, Earl Evans and many others, who got into the fledgling speed equipment business. Most of them concentrated on equipment for the Ford flathead. Racing—at the Lakes and later at Bonneville and the drags—was the crucible. If you won, people flocked to you and *your* equipment. Articles and advertisements in *Hot Rod* spread the word. But there were a lot of speed secrets that weren't publicized. Barney is particularly sensitive about the use of special racing fuels. In a "Now it can be told" way, he related an interesting tale:

"Rollie Mack, who was the advertising manager of Petersen Publications, came into my office one day," said Barney. "He wanted to know what I planned to do with my ad (in *Hot Rod*) for September. I told him, 'It depends on you fellas. You never mention when somebody sets a record at the lakes whether they're using nitromethane or hydrazine chloride or what they were doing. Those things are left out.'

"So Rollie said, 'Why don't you write a letter?'" Barney replied that as a manufacturer, it would seem like sour grapes if he wrote something. "Then Rollie said, 'Write a feature article.'"

BATCHELOR ARCHIVES/RON KELLOG COLLECTION

COURTESY DON MONTGOMERY

Published in the November, 1950, issue of *Hot Rod* and titled, "The Pros and Cons of Super Fuel," it became the first article Barney ever wrote. But it wasn't easy to get it published. Barney took the first draft to Wally Parks, who "...had a kind of sour look on his face when he saw it." Parks read it and told Barney to "...embellish it a little." Barney revised the piece and brought it back the next day. He recalls, "Don Francisco was the technical editor; they came out of their offices and didn't say anything. Then Rollie Mack showed up and said, 'What are you doing here Barney?'"

Navarro explained he'd written the fuel article and had given it to Wally Parks. He told Mack, "I'm waiting to see what Wally's going to do with it, so I'll know what to do with my next ad."

"I knew that I had 'em by the short hair," Navarro says today with a chuckle.

"There was kind of a conspiracy going on. Vic Edelbrock was using fuel and he'd been using it at Bonneville, keeping it secret. The year I was inducted into the Dry Lakes Hall of Fame, Bobby Meeks [who built engines for Edelbrock] was on the stage, too. He confessed that they did a lot of things—that they ran nitro in the midget that used to run at Gilmore, they turned the engine backwards so that it would load the inside wheel instead of the outside wheel.

"So I was the agitator at that time, and that article was the beginning of it."

Barney's 1/6th page ad appeared adjacent to his article on page 23 of the same issue. Interestingly, the headline states: "Only Navarro heads give you compression without choking off or restricting the gas passage. Maximum compression is necessary when using straight alcohol fuel."

"When the advertiser's copies were sent out, ahead of when newsstands and subscribers received them, Edelbrock raised hell with Petersen. Petersen agreed to let Bobby Meeks write an article that soft-pedaled the effects of nitro-methane. [I think this is the one that appeared under Don

Francisco's name in HRM in February, 1951.] He also pointed out that you couldn't use more than 25 percent [nitro]. Ed Winfield had been egging those guys on for some time. He said, 'Why are you guys just tipping the can for 25 percent? Go all the way. Use straight nitromethane.'

"I think eventually some of them did. Tony Capana sold a purple-colored nitromethane fuel mix with vegetable dye in it that they called 'the purple passion.' But he didn't tell everybody it was nitromethane. Going back to the photos in *Hop Up* in 1951, that was the first time I'd ever run oxygen injection. There's one on the front carburetor and one on the back carburetor. But if you look closely [at the picture], the back carburetor's gone. The injector is still hanging there. It backfired; the oxygen continued to flow, and it turned the carburetor into dust. The exhaust pipe was just sprayed with that stuff. But it didn't harm the engine. All I had to do was get another carburetor. The fire when out with the last pump of the Pyrene fire extinguisher. I eventually got that car up to 137 mph at another meet."

Barney wasn't against using fuel; he objected to the inconsistency that arose because the rules didn't specifically separate fuel users from non-users, and he called for special classes to level the playing field. Interestingly, it took years before the matter was finally resolved, and the NHRA found itself on the wrong side of the issue for several years.

In his era, most competitors didn't do much theorizing in writing. Barney charitably opines that most of them didn't have the background. "They really didn't understand the principles," he says. "Some of those early manifolds (that collectors cherish today) really didn't work."

Ford factory engineers understood how to maximize the 180-degree firing order and harness their engine's impulses effectively. Barney's first really successful manifolds built on those principles rather than trying entirely new manifold configurations, like many less successful rivals. He further improved the dual- and later triple-manifold's plenum chamber to maximize mixture flow.

Navarro obviously made the most of his schooling. In the depths of the Depression, he attended Eagle Rock High School, and he also went to night classes at Glendale High. He's quick to point out that, in those days, Glendale High School had "...one of the best machine shops in the State of California." Barney laments that it was torn down 20 years ago, and he's saddened that so few places teach quality machine work today.

Through the late Forties, Barney developed several manifolds (duals, triples and GMC blower) and head designs (regular and high-dome) for the '39-'53 flathead; his shop also did considerable machine work and built engines for street and racing clients. And he remained an active racer. Barney was (and still is) proud of the fact that despite Tom Beatty's frequently blown engines, Beatty set a number of records in his belly tank, running a series of blown flatheads in the high 180s with Navarro equipment.

Barney himself was known for reliable engines that "stayed together." In July, 1952, he authored a memorable *Hot Rod* magazine article entitled, "My Fordomatic Takes A Beating." Navarro built a 284-cid (3 5/16 x 4 1/8) full-race motor that he ran on the street in his '51 Ford Tudor. At the 21,000-mile mark, Navarro explained to readers how his 170-bhp engine ran coolly and sweetly on the streets but would show a clean pair of heels to Olds and Cadillac overheads when challenged. One of the illustrations shows Barney walking alongside the idling Ford at the Santa Ana drag strip—graphic proof of just how flexible the engine was.

By the mid-Fifties, Barney offered a four-barrel "Duo-Duplex" manifold for the '49-'53 Ford and Mercury V8s that used a then-contemporary '55 Thunderbird Holley Quad-jet carburetor and an oil bath air cleaner from an F-8 Ford truck. He claimed this setup—which he admired when Ray Crawford refined it for the Mexican road-race Lincolns—gave a 15-bhp increase, using the stock distributor. Barney also offered a McCulloch supercharger to further enhance the four-barrel and claimed a 5psi boost was achievable. Unfortunately, Ford went to overhead valves in 1954, and Chevrolet followed with a superior V8 that quickly became a hot rodder's delight. By 1957, demand for his equipment had slackened. The day of the flathead was over. Barney had to look for other income streams.

Barney says, in hindsight, the high cost of developing equipment for the Chevy and other overheads was a barrier for his small firm. In the early Sixties, he built a heart-lung machine that was used by many hospitals, and he later developed a series of electrically powered, lightweight aluminum concrete-cutting saws. But racing never left his imagination. In 1966, with limited financial backing, Barney built an AirResearch turbocharged and injected stock-block Nash Rambler six engine for the Indianapolis 500 that developed a remarkable 640 bhp at 7000 rpm—without a cross-flow head!

In 1985, a chance meeting with Don Ferguson, Sr., a long-time Bonneville racer, provided the impetus for Barney to get back into manufacturing a limited amount of his cherished speed equipment. You can order genuine Navarro equipment today simply by calling (818) 241-6644. Barney is still offering heads, manifolds and brackets made with some of the same molds he's used for decades. He's also still using the same foundry in Long Beach, except "...now I'm dealing with the grandsons of the original owners."

I had to ask Barney for a few comments on some of the leading racing lights of his era. He's quick to say these are just his opinions, but when you're dealing with a legend, you take him seriously. Pete Clark and Rex Mays were the drivers he most respected; Ed Winfield, Pierre (Pete) Bertrand and Clay Smith were his favorite cam grinders. Barney wasn't a fan of the Ardun flathead conversions, but he concedes they developed considerable horsepower. "That big rocker arm setup and the long pushrods are futile," he says. "Why not stick the cam up there?" Navarro loves pop-up pistons, insisting that with his special flathead pop-up heads, the resulting combustion chamber is not unlike a Chrysler Hemi's. He's always believed in matching ports and smoothing the way fuel travels. "Nothing is better than a graceful path from carb to valve," insists Barney, pulling out mechanical drawings from the 1940s to prove his point.

Sitting in Barney's office, listening to him expound on theories of valve timing, air flow, superchargers and how to build a better flathead block (sorry, I know you'd like to hear it, but we've run out of space), you feel as though you're in the presence of a retired college physics professor rather than an elderly lakes racer/machinist who became a speed equipment manufacturer. Although he never became a millionaire like the Edelbrocks, Weiands and Granatellis, hot rodding is far richer for the presence of Barney Navarro.

DICK FLINT ROADSTER

This magazine cover car and Pebble Beach winner also put two kids through college. Co-eds looked different in '51, didn't they?

NOVEMBER 1951

The Dick Flint Roadster appeared on *Hop Up*'s cover in November 1951. It has been photographed, painted, illustrated, storied, revered, copied, and now restored, as is the fashion, to a higher level of excellence than it ever had originally. Good. Another product of DBO Motorsports (Don Orosco, Brad Hand, et. al.), it wrangled first place at Pebble Beach from the likes of the McGee roadster, So-Cal Speed Shop and Bruce Meyer. Not easily done.

The slippery little A-Bone had the typical famous-roadster life: Inspired guys build car, owner turns it in a short time, it is sold again, this time to a Hop Up type guy who "got it" even back then, and kept it for a hundred years. It will always be the "Flint" car, but Duane Kofoed was its caretaker for over 25 years. Think about it, man: Whose car was it, really? We think the description of the cars ought to be "Spencer-East-Meyer," "Xydias-Travis-Orosco," "McGee-Scritchfield-Meyer," etc. Those monikers don't flow easily in hot rod jive talk, though, so maybe it's OK that those of us who care, know.

Kofoed, when asked why he ever sold it said, "I had two kids to put through college…it bugged me for a long time but I got over it…. When I look at how good those kids turned out, well, it's all OK now."

Not many hot rod roadsters have facilitated success stories, have they, boys?

Taking full advantage of Barney Navarro's flathead speed equipment, Tom Beatty's tank set speed records on the lakes for five years in a row, beginning in 1951. He had similar success on the salt.

TOM BEATTY'S TANK

By Dave Simard

DECEMBER 1951

Undoubtedly a book could be written on Tom Beatty's accomplishments between 1951 and 1963, when he piloted his record-setting tank at El Mirage and Bonneville.

The '51 season first put Beatty in the record books with a 188-mph run—the fastest speed ever on the lakes! Beatty dominated the lakes continuously, setting the fastest speed for five years in a row. The same was true at Bonneville, where Tom regularly set records in B, C, and D Lakester classes.

It was the advanced design and construction, using the knowledge of both Beatty and Barney Navarro, that put this tank out front for 13 seasons. The original design changed little through most of the Fifties, though Beatty ran numerous flathead engines. In 1957, he rebuilt the tank with supercharged Oldsmobile power; and in 1960 Tom lengthened it to accommodate an Olds transmission that was modified to connect directly with the Halibrand rear. Beatty captured the D Lakester record at 243.43 mph in 1963 with this arrangement. It was his last racing season.

The tank was stored in Beatty's garage until Tom Geradi purchased it in 1983, two years before Tom Beatty passed away. Mark Dees bought the disassembled tank from Geradi in 1992, but he made little progress before his untimely death in 1997. At this point, I purchased the tank intending to locate the original parts and rebuild it as Beatty had last raced it.

The tank currently has the original blue paint from 1961, with the "Tom Beatty Automotive Engineering" lettering blazing across the canopy. The tank is not running, but when time permits, I'll return it to running condition.

EDDIE MILLER 'LINER

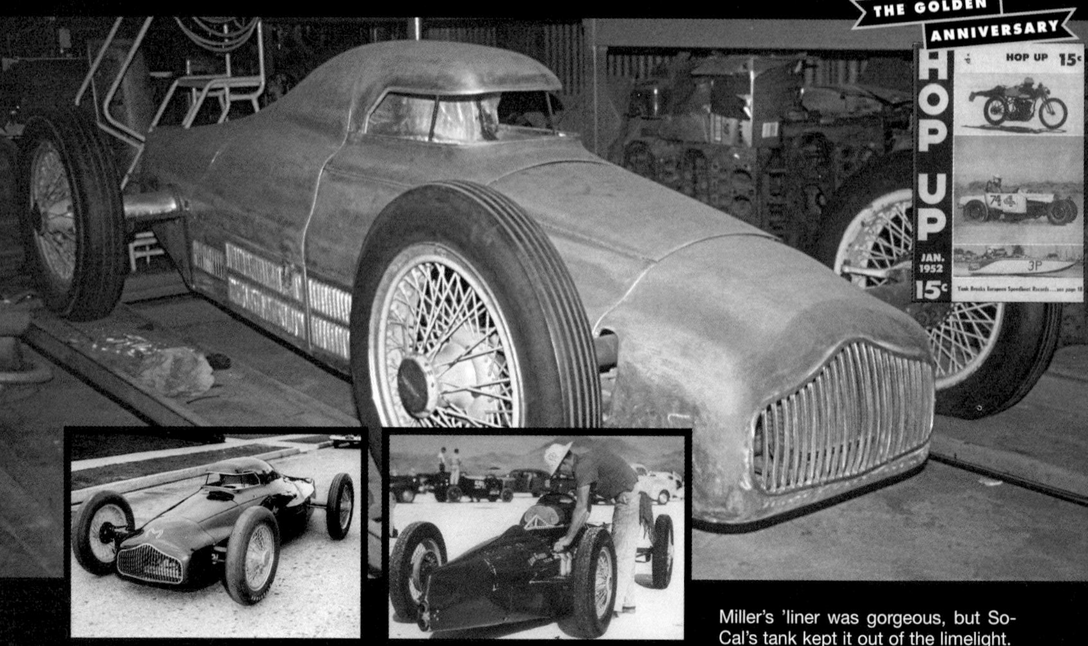

Miller's 'liner was gorgeous, but So-Cal's tank kept it out of the limelight.

JANUARY 1952

This car should be more famous, more notable, more publicized, than it is.

Eddie Miller Sr. was a riding mechanic (mechanician), fabricator and tuner who kept Duesenberg racecars in front in the Teens and Twenties. His son Jr. is the person responsible for the beautiful design and fabrication of the streamliner we see here, running a Pontiac flathead six. Current owner Don Ferguson (he's the cat who's making the complete Ardun head sets) let us "over the moat" to actually lay hands on this piece and explore its character, taking advantage of the owner's familiarity with, and respectful awe for, the car.

He tells us that there wasn't much racing success, because the So-Cal tank was in the same class, and those rascals kept upping the ante each time Miller would pick up a few miles per hour. That's racin.'

While the liner's beauty is apparent, the beauty (excellence) of its fabrication has to be explained. The car might have been the product of the most anal-'80s street rod builder in the country. Its custom cast motor mounts; filed, ground and polished welds; symmetry; balance, and function are pure '80s. Who was this guy?!

The car's history gets a little clouded in the later Fifties, but we recently read a vintage racing newsletter from 1973 where the late Mark Dees had offered the car for sale "complete but apart" for $700. He got only one call, and he said, "Bring a trailer and some money. You're buyin' it." It got to the Ferguson collection sometime since, and although we've been teased with sightings here and there over the years, we think it's going public. Full restoration, complete with beer-bottle brown paint. (Ya had ta be there!)

The early photos demo the fine finish, while the current restoration-in-progress shots reveal the class that was buried beneath the lacquer. Huzzah, you Hop Up Guys. Take off your Stroker hat. This is one of the biggies.

RALPH JILEK '40

THE GOLDEN ANNIVERSARY

Don Orosco is bringing the Jilek '40 back to its original look.

FEBRUARY 1952

The Ralph Jilek '40 convertible showed up as Custom of the Month in February 1952.

A Valley Custom project, it differed from the current version only in appointments: It originally had 16-inch wheels, wide whitewalls, full wheel discs, spots and '46 Chevy bumpers. While this is one of the four *Hop Up* Golden Anniversary cars currently in the Don Orosco collection, it has not yet had the "healing hand" laid on it. Don acquired the car in almost-restored condition but opted to give it his own treatment, probably agreeing with *Hop Up* that the original configuration is the righteous choice.

Maybe we can lose the way-out nerfies, huh Don?

MARCH 1952

This piece was a *Hot Rod* cover car as well as a *Hop Up* feature at about the same time. No wonder in hell. What better captures the spirit of hot rodding than this Archie/Jake/Finkmobile with the missing fenders, cool stance and attitude?

In this "where are they now?" look at the cars, how could it be better than: "It is still in the family, it is used regularly, and its look remains the same"? A tribute to a dad who must've been a real Hop Up Guy—a character by all reviews, blessed with sons that feel about the car the way Red did.

Few of the cars in this chapter have not changed ownership. Keep it in the family!

TOM (RED) HYNES T TOURING

THE GOLDEN ANNIVERSARY

The rare rod that's still all in the family.

Eddie Dye Roadster

THE GOLDEN ANNIVERSARY

Jim Fuller's roadster (above) has the nose, but Tom Branch's car (right) has the chassis, body and title from the original Eddie Dye car.

MARCH '52 COVER

This car is what one of our mentors calls a "custom roadster"—not a hardcore lakes car, but one executed with beauty as primal a motivation as was performance. This style has inspired plenty of projects along the way, including some fairly recent ones.

In *Hop Up 2000* we mentioned that there was some apparent controversy about the "real" Eddie Dye car, and *Hop Up* still agrees that the chassis, body, title, etc., live with Tom Branch, shown here. But the original front of the car, including windshield, hood and snoot still exist (everyone agrees). We turned it up in the garage of and on the front of Jim Fuller's roadster, also shown here. We make no certifiable statement about what's what here, except that after talking to all parties, it appears that Fuller's car was built around the hood 'n' snoot 'n' 'shield, and Branch's car was the car remodeled with the vital front end forsaken. We THINK this is how it was and we THINK all parties agree. But it doesn't really matter. Que sera sera. All the players are Hop Up Guys. Nuff said.

A recent event makes this all notable: DBO has acquired the car from Branch, and a restored roadster is immanent.

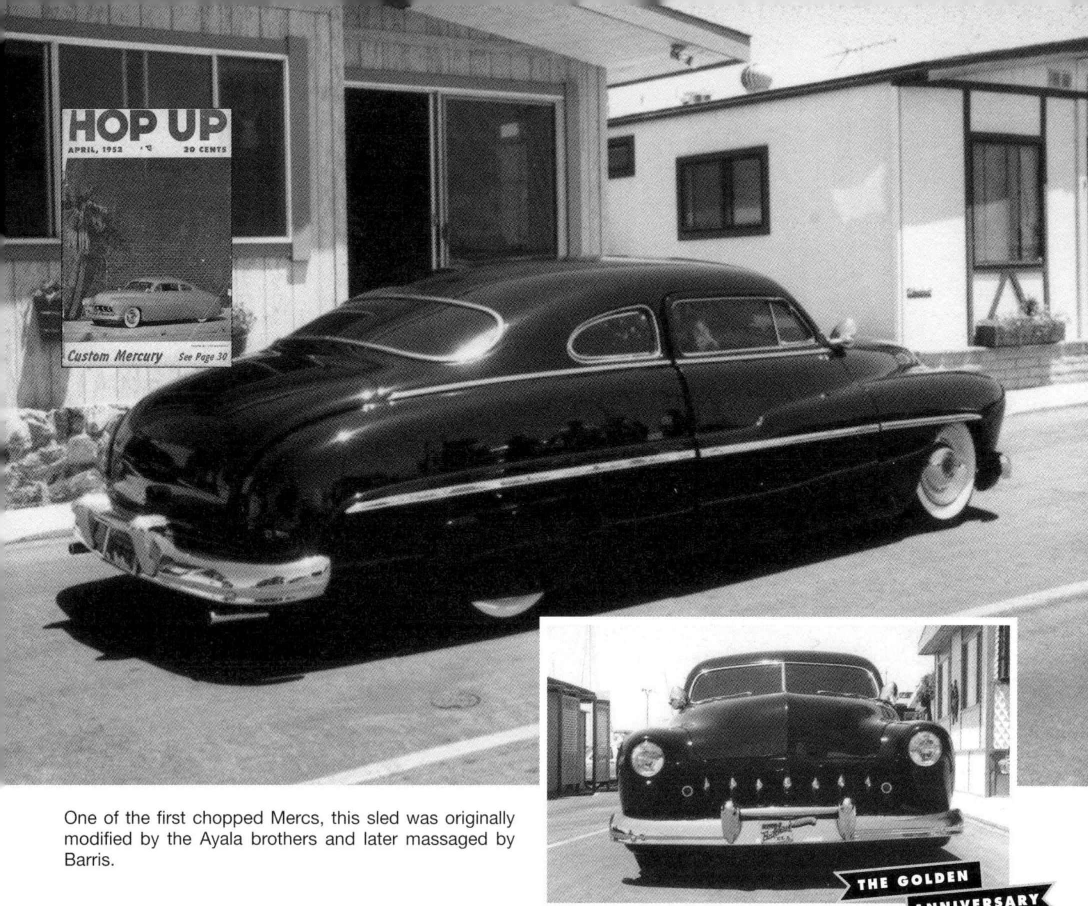

One of the first chopped Mercs, this sled was originally modified by the Ayala brothers and later massaged by Barris.

THE GOLDEN ANNIVERSARY

WALLY WELCH MERC

By Joe Eddy

APRIL '52 COVER

This 1950 Mercury was purchased new by Wally Welch and customized by the Ayala Brothers. The top was chopped, head- and taillights frenched, frame "C'd," door handles removed and solenoids installed. All emblems were removed, and DeSoto grille teeth were installed in the frenched shell. The Merc was finished in lime green.

The car, one of the first chopped Mercs, was considered among the top 10 radical customs of the '50s. It was featured in several magazines and awarded the "Best Custom" title at the 1951 Pan Pacific Autorama.

In late 1951, Barris Kustoms added two teeth to the grille and refinished it in deep-deep purple. It was then named "Purple Rage."

Purple Rage was sold in 1953, enjoyed by its second owner for two years, then put in storage when Uncle Sam called. Over 30 years later, it was found and purchased by present owner Joe Eddy. During a three-year restoration, the car was stripped to bare metal, the body massaged where necessary, the chrome replated, and the running gear rebuilt with a Chevy 400 engine, Turbo Hydro trans, 9-inch Ford rearend and power steering. In 1987, Purple Rage was reborn in a lustrous new Kandy Grape coating.

THE GOLDEN ANNIVERSARY

HOLY ROLLER

Love at first sight: Burns knew in '52 this car would someday be his.

By Burns Berryman

MAY 1952

Larry Ernst, a Catholic priest from Ohio, purchased this '51 Chevy hardtop new and took it immediately to Barris Kustoms in Los Angeles, originally for a mild reworking. But one thing led to another, and Larry decided to go the full kustom route. When the car was finished, it came to Don Le'One's home in Berkley, Michigan. He and Larry took the car to shows throughout the country. I first saw it in 1952 in Birmingham, Michigan. They asked me if I wanted a ride to Ted's Drive-In in Pontiac, and while riding in the car, I told them that someday I'd own the car.

After following the car for almost 30 years, I purchased it in 1980 and returned it to the original purple version done by Barris in '51. The second version, done in 1952, had minor body changes, new paint, and a Wayne 12-port 270 GMC engine. Then in 1953 it returned to Barris' shop for the version you see in the Keith Ashley clone.

After purchasing the car I was able to locate Larry, by then a retired monsignor priest, and we became very good friends. He was kind enough to give me many of the trophies the car won over the years. Larry passed away in 1993, and he left us an artist's rendering, done by Jim Rich of Ann Arbor, of the Barris shop with both versions of the car in front. I redid the car for my handicapped son, who was 20 when I purchased it. It has been shown only once since 1993. I enjoy just owning it, along with my other cars.

Ray Vega Custom Ford

THE GOLDEN ANNIVERSARY

The convertible sedan is on its way back to the way it was on the '52 cover.

MAY 1952 COVER

Tony Handler has had the '38 convertible sedan with the '40 snoot on it since 1962. Makes it kinda hard to call it the Ray Vega car, huh?

He found it in an impound yard behind a cafe in Pearblossom, a diner/gas station combo that you probably still go through on your way to El Mirage. The front end of the car was damaged, so he needed some new '40 sheetmetal. It was upon installing the replacement parts that he realized the original fenders had been lengthened by a pro (Valley Custom): hammer-welded so fine you could barely detect the graft. Then there was the 5-inch channeling and 3-inch chop. Scraps of the original tooled upholstery material turned up, and a little research defined the car as the May 1952 *Hop Up* cover car.

Serendipity enters the story, as can happen when you've had a car almost 40 years. Tony met a guy at one of the early Long Beach T Meets at Hamilton Bowl who had owned the car after Vega and still had the top latches. The top had been pulled off to dazzle some chicks on a boozy summer night, and when they got back the next day the top was gone. Latches were then removed and stored. Tony met a bartender who had owned the car BEFORE Vega; he found the pillar/dividers at Valley Ford Obsolete with the Valley Maroon paint still on them. Some things are meant to be. Tony had removed all the windows, tracks and relevant hardware because he wanted to weld the car into a phaeton, so he gave the parts to the guy who had bought Valley Custom. About a hundred years later, Tony came across the guy, who still had the parts in the same box, and the parts were returned, no charge!

Hogged-out wheel wells, a dozen different engines, and the hard-charge of a Hop Up kinda guy have given the car a history of unforgettable escapades. Today it is being restored to the almost-1952 period; the subtle modifications Tony has made only improve the balance of the car. It is triple black with a hot flathead, un-tooled leather with 4-inch pleats, banjo steering wheel, and the bumpers have become Lincoln instead of Ford. We expect a full feature in *Hop Up Volume III.*

THE GOLDEN ANNIVERSARY

TRIPLE THREAT: THE DAL PORTO ROADSTER

Jack Hageman originally fashioned this roadster's unique nose, grille and bodywork; and current owner Kerry Horan is restoring it to its original glory.

By Kerry Horan

JULY 1952

Some cars achieve fame through their good looks. Others make a name for themselves in action on the lakes or at the digs. The Dal Porto roadster did all three. Built in 1951, it was clocked at 153 mph on the dry lakes and reached 118 mph at the end of the quarter-mile. The July, 1952 *Hop Up* cover car also won its class at the Oakland Roadster show in 1953.

Its chassis and distinctive nose, grille and bodywork were created by the renowned Jack Hageman, while John Errecalde completed the engine and other work for owner Albert Dal Porto.

During a run at El Mirage in 1953, the car was damaged in a rollover. Dal Porto stored the car until the early 1970s, when it was acquired by Carl Schmid of Stockton, California. Ownership passed to Don Orosco in 1993 and to Kerry Horan in 1999. Horan is currently restoring the car to its original condition.

the JAZZY SPECIAL

Time capsule: Chuck Sarno (left) drove this track-nose T at the lakes and on the strip in the mid-Fifties, bought it in the Sixties and began its restoration in the Nineties.

By Chuck Sarno

SEPTEMBER 1952

In 1946, Jim "Jazzy" Nelson and his brother, Paul, started modifying their 1927 T roadster in Culver City, California. During 1948 and 1949, Jazzy ran the car in the Mojave Timing Association, where he and Paul set a B Class Roadster record at 141.06 mph in 1948.

Jazzy entered the car in the first National Roadster Show in Oakland in 1949 and then again in 1950. In the 1950 show, the car placed third in "Construction-Lake Division" and second in "Originality-Lake Division."

Soon after, Jazzy sold the car to Lee Titus, owner of Lee's Speed Shop in Santa Monica. Lee installed a 296-cubic-inch flathead, and in 1951 took the car to Bonneville. He went 151 on the salt; and Dean Moon, who also drove this car in '51 at Bonneville, topped out at over 152 mph. This marked the first time Dean had gone over 150.

Around 1954, the Palms Garage, a shop on Motor Avenue in the small L.A. community of Palms, acquired the car. The next year yours truly drove it at El Mirage and the San Fernando Drag Strip. From 1958 until 1963 the car sat in storage at the Palms Garage. Then in 1963, I bought the car (for somewhere between $250 and $500), and put it in storage until 1995, when we started a complete restoration.

From the top: Triple-duty roadster ran as a Coupes Club entry; restoration uses November 1952 *Hop Up* as a visual guide and to pinpoint the time. This roadster, like most hot rods, had several later lives.

THE DON FERRARA ROADSTER

NOVEMBER 1952

The Don Ferrara roadster may be one of the most featured roadsters of its time. We've seen two *Hot Rod* Mag features, three *Hop Up* entries and maybe a *Rod & Custom* shot, too. Sometime after Ferrara, the car went to Bill Roland, whose re-do copped a *Hot Rod* feature. Roland is the guy who eventually bought the Ivo T Bucket and "personalized" it, too.

At the L.A. Roadsters Father's Day show last June, Don Ferarra himself and the current owner, Richard Baron, presented *Hop Up* with the attached photos from then—and now—and blew us righteously flat away. Don, who by the looks of him must have been three years old when he built the car, has been more involved in boats and airplanes in recent years. He is bemused by the hoopla, but he recognizes the historic significance of the car, and his exploits with it, including various historical photos of Tom (Stroker) Medley in the car.

Richard Baron, who has owned the car since 1973, is in the midst of a complete restoration, using "November 1952 *Hop Up*" as his reference point. Our kinda guy.

Clockwise, from top left: Don is parked on the bluffs near where Jim Stark and Buzzie made their "fatal" chickie run!; Baron restoration is/will be correct down to the smallest detail. Assistance from Ferrara himself, Medley, the photos, and several magazine features make it attainable; flame licks are from an after-life in the '70s. They will go in favor of November 1952 paint scheme seen in *Hop Up*; Great original photos, like this one from the Ferrara collection, leave no mysteries to solve in the engine compartment; lots of nice detail and the fine finish helped make the car a standout of its time.

THE GOLDEN ANNIVERSARY

THE So-Cal COUPE

Xydias and Batchelor. The streamliner, the tank, the logo, the legends. We can't do the history as well as the big boys, Boys, but some of it is our own. Batchelor, you see, was an original editor of *Hop Up*. Xydias is currently a pal of ours.

Now, the cats at DBO Motorsports are Hop Up Guys along with the rest of us—moaning, head-shaking romantics who, because of opportunity, wherewithal, and tenacity are bringing another icon from "the day" back for our pleasure.

Jim Travis, a major story in his own right, campaigned the coupe for many years. He fell under the persuasive spell of Don Orosco, who is restoring the car for a "coupes" debut at Pebble Beach 2001. This summer it will be facing off with the Pearson Brothers coupe, Chrisman and Duncan, Stone, Woods and Cook and Lordy knows what all else, on the green at that nickeled, silvered, cloisonne'd, lacquered-up deal in Monterey. Competition Coupes. God! America is great.

The So-Cal Coupe appeared in *Hop Up* in the early days. Here it is again, at the beginning of its restoration, blown apart, diced, sliced and pondered. Don says he wishes he'd gotten the car just four weeks before the show. Then he could be sure the restoration would be authentic! The inherent time-squeeze compromises would have mimed the practices of the racers during its long history. As it is, he'll have too much time to do it well. Like all hot rods and racecars, there is conjecture about what period to pick for the restoration. These cars are always a work in progress (Hop Up Guys are hep to that one), and some really fun and funny techniques were used: bubble gum welds, angle iron brackets and…you know.

Restoration Team Leader Brad Hand, with the artful assistance of metalman Ole Eriksson, have the car in a submissive stance as reflected in the accompanying photos. There is time for the completion of the project, and we applaud Don and his team for selecting a Hop Up car in celebration of our 50th. Right?

Across town, the So-Cal Speed Shop may have some competition brewing, too, not the least of which is the Pearson Brothers Coupe, restored there about seven years ago and not showing any wear. They're probably not threatened, though. They can't "lose" either way!

Watch the Hop Up web page (www.hopupmag.com) in September for the results.

Feast your eyes on an inside peek at history—the So-Cal coupe blown apart during its restoration. With the car stripped like this you can see the kind of handiwork that went into a lakes coupe back in the day. When it's finished, the coupe will make its debut on the finely manicured lawns of Pebble Beach. Dean would be proud.

HOP UP *Magazine* 5-WINDOW BUILD UP

UPDATE 2001: NO FREE PARTS, NO SHAMELESS PLUGS

Since we last commiserated, la bombe is fully blown apart. The foundation is the chassis, so we drag it to Jake for straightening as necessary, motor mounts to double for flathead and 283, stay-rods, hairpins, boxing. All this to be done with the intent to just make the piece functional and throw it back together, albeit with more structural refinements than it had when the Surgers were floggin' it all over So Cal.

The attached shot will demonstrate just how cool basic frame work can be: gorgeous welds, thoughtful parts design, and sound framework done without sacrifice to the gods of modernity. Just the idea that this thing can swap out its Chevy 283 for a flattie—at will—because the Chevy motor mounts were designed to bolt to flathead motor mount bases, makes us appreciate the possibilities in the future.

With the frame done, all the suspension parts had to come apart again, get sandblasted for primer and satin finish from rattle cans, then get laid out for final assembly. The 283 engine has been rebuilt for months; the '39 trans (with Lincoln Zephyr gears) was rebuilt by Joe Mac, and we had the '40 banjo rearend redone with a new 3:54 gear set (which came from a *Hop Up* advertiser. We paid for it. No shameless plugs, man).

Rebush this, reline that, paint up one of these, order a pair of those...crap! This buildin' a beater ain't any different than painted, plated, trimmed and rimmed, except there is no paint, plate, trim or rims!

In order to push the envelope of Hop Up expression, ya gotta have a gag. You know, some thing that makes it different; says the guy has been thinking in a world that has gotten on to 5-windows in a big way. We think we have the gag; and although it doesn't show up on the Charlie Cruz illustration, we'll invite you to kick our tires when you see the car at this year's Rattle Can Nationals.

You Need TO JOIN THE SURGERS!

By Doug Clark

Driving up Interstate 99 in the hot summer heat of '61, I spotted the 5-window Deuce coupe with a "For Sale" sign on it. After shelling out $300 in hard saved cash, I had the pink slip in hand and drove the coupe to Tahoe with my friend riding shotgun.

It was orange with spots of primer and had an oil-smoking Studebaker V8 for power. The engine blew up there in the high altitude, so we had to rent a tow-bar and hitch for the trip home. Once back, I pulled the engine and ended up buying a rear-end-crashed '40 Ford sedan with a small-block Chevy. I pulled the engine and tranny and plopped it into the coupe. I took to the streets and ran it around Glendale, looking over my shoulder at all times for Marinelli, the bad-ass motorcycle cop who loved to ticket teen hot rodders.

It was while tuning it one night in the carport that Paul Freund stuck his mug under the hood and said, "You need to join the Surgers Car Club. I have a Deuce just like this one, plus we have a '34 Vicky sedan that's our project car." I joined the club and got my Surgers jacket and plate, identifying our shorts when we cruised Bob's in Glendale or Toluca Lake.

Writing this has brought back so many nostalgic thoughts. Like weekly meetings ending with a run to Bob's, shooting wet paper straw wrappings up to the acoustic ceiling while sipping cherry cokes and scarfing Big Boys and fries. "American Graffiti" happening before the movie.

The next step for the coupe was to take it from street legal to drag legal. Hello hand-made headers, slicks, Moon tank, and a hot little short-block that measured only 272 cubes (265 block, 1/8 over). Plus six Strombergs, straight linkage (no pussy progressive on my engine). Believe it or not, I ran the stock '40 tranny and rearend and NEVER blew either one. Sheared a few axle keys, though.

The coupe ran in the 12's at around 108. It won B-Gas many times. By the end of its racing days, it had blue Plexiglas side windows that came about because of a mental error on my part. Because everyone was into "weight-transfer" (front end up, rear end down), I thought it would be great to pull the front shocks and let the car shift its weight on its own as it went down the strip. Well, in the final class race, the coupe's front end went airborne. It drifted to the dirt, taking out the timing lights as it slowly dropped to the right side, then drifted back onto the strip, sliding in big doughnuts until it came to a stop. That's how the coupe got the ground-down rain gutter, which takes us back to where this started.

I got a call from my old Surger buddy, Paul Freund, about a guy who bought my old coupe. He knew it was mine because he looked at the rain gutter and said, "Yep, that's Doug Clark's old coupe all right." When I first heard about the '32, it didn't excite me too much. But when Paul died a few months later, a tear or two ran down my cheeks as I thought of the story, and what those years meant to me. I can tell you this. It is a really good, warm feeling knowing where it is today and how it's going to look when Mark is finished with it.

Take good care of my baby, Mark. You've got a good one!

Race Cars

"The Saga of the Roaring Road" was written by Fred Wagner, a forebear of the starters and flagmen who have officiated motor races since the turn of the century. He'd been conscripted as a starter in early races because of his experience as starter for bicycle races. Thus his career, passion, and the book.

It really is a "Saga" ("a continuing story," according to *Funk and Wagnall's*) that carries through to today, with the archaic, but romantic iron seen in this chapter. *Hop Up* has gathered some then and some now, lacking only the "Roar" that, well, you gotta be there to appreciate.

It was a good century, no?

BATCHELOR ARCHIVES/RON KELLOG COLLECTION

RODDERS GO R

By Jim Chini

Hot rodding and oval-track racing have been joined at the hip for almost 90 years. This relationship dates back to the early 20th Century when testosterone-laden boys would strip down dad's cast-off Model T or Chevrolet to go roaring around cornfields and vacant lots, pretending to be Ralph DePalma. Throughout this union, the vehicle of choice has been the roadster, ineptly defined in a 1938 Funk & Wagnall's Dictionary as "A strongly built automobile-adapted for use on ordinary roads, rather than for racing." This definition probably earned the company the 1938 "Unclear on the Concept" award!

The choice of the roadster was a no-brainer. The cars were light-weight and, when stripped down, had an "almost-race-car" look to them. There was also the wind-in-the-hair/bugs-on-the-teeth syndrome to consider.

Almost as soon as the Great War ended, companies bearing such names as Frontenac, Roof and Rajo began offering "street" versions of their racing equipment; and that stripped-down roadster could now not only look fast but go fast as well. Although some of these aftermarket companies were located east of the Rockies, it took only a few years for sunny Southern California to become the center of the universe for this industry. Impromptu street drags and an occasional trip to the dry lakebeds became quite popular, and it wasn't long before the idea of longer races took flower.

Since there were no five- or 10-mile straight-line venues available, someone decided to bend that straight line into a circle and do it just like the real race cars did.

ALL PHOTOS COURTESY OF THE CHINI COLLECTION

OUNDY-ROUND PART ONE

From the top: Brothers Ed and Bud Winfield manufactured some of the most sought-after cams, carburetors and Model A conversions in rodding history. They also collaborated on a pair of incredible eight-cylinder engines for the Indianapolis 500, the last of which, a DOHC V configuration, would become known as the Novi. Few remember that Ed was a highly successful roadster and sprint-car driver in the 1920s. This photo, from 1927, shows him at Ascot in his Fronty-T-powered bobtail with some very trick Winfield Bros. induction; in 1938, Floyd Roberts of Van Nuys, California, became one of the earliest roadster racing graduates to win the Indianapolis 500 and finished out the year as the A.A.A. national driving champion. Unfortunately, his success was short-lived, as he was killed at Indianapolis the following year. This photo was taken at the one-mile Oakland, California, Speedway in 1935 with Floyd at the wheel of Earl Haskell's immaculate Miller-powered sprint car.

Top: Karl Young was a roadster regular until switching to the then-new midget cars in 1934. He took to the small cars like a duck to water; and in 1936, he won the Gilmore Stadium championship. "King Karl" was a great showman and became a darling of the fans. He stayed out of racing for several years during WWII but returned to his winning ways at Gilmore in 1946 and retired after the 1950 season. This photo from Gilmore in 1940 shows him in Charlie Allen's Offenhauser, which was the first complete car built by Frank Kurtis. **Bottom (left to right)**: Bob Swanson is considered by experts to be one of the greatest midget-car drivers of all time. His transition from roadsters to the small cars in 1934 was seamless. He was National Midget Association champion in 1935, won the Gilmore Grand Prix in 1934 and 1938, and is the all-time leader in main-event wins at Gilmore Stadium. He was killed at Toledo, Ohio, barely two weeks after finishing sixth in the 1940 Indianapolis 500. This photo, taken at Gilmore in 1935, shows Bob behind the wheel of Danny Hogan's spotless Offenhauser; Eddie Meyer, Jr., although not as famous a driver as his younger brother, Louis, was a formidable competitor in roadsters and sprint cars during the 1920s. He owned racecars into the 1960s but was much better known in the hot rod community for his line of high-quality speed equipment. The Redlands Special is a car that he built, owned, and, until around 1926, drove. He is posed here at Legion Ascot Speedway in the fast little OHV Rajo-powered machine sometime during the 1929 season.

ALL PHOTOS COURTESY OF THE CHINI COLLECTION

Suddenly, big-time auto racing had an entry-level division where young men could get the feel of wheel-to-wheel competition without having to invest major money in a full-blown race car. The first races were improvised and disorganized affairs, done just for the fun of it at temporary and primitive venues. However, it was only a short time before they were discovered by some "legitimate" race promoters. These boys soon found themselves racing on real racetracks, with paid spectators and, if they were lucky, maybe for some prize money.

By the early 1930s roadster racing was well established in California, with nearly two-dozen tracks from San Diego in the south up through the great Central Valley and the San Francisco Bay Area to the north, presenting races on any given Sunday, year-round. The sport had caught on in the other sun-belt states as well, and was beginning to be seen on a limited basis in the Midwest. Although the Model A Ford-based Cragar and HAL conversions would dominate the sport up to WWII, the debut of Henry's V8 in 1932 ushered in a whole new phase for the aftermarket industry and the racers who patronized it.

The Second World War brought this phase of roadster racing to a halt in 1942. It would return with a vengeance in 1946, but that is a story for another time.

We have picked out just a few of the men who drove roadsters before WWII and went on to become famous in other areas of the auto racing game. Some you may have heard of, others not, but all made an indelible mark on the fabric of American auto racing history.'

From the top: The most famous racer to come out of Southern California roadsters prior to WWII was the great Rex Mays. He was three times Pacific Coast A.A.A. sprint-car champ in 1934, '35 and '48, Mid-West title holder in 1936 and '37, and National Champion in 1940 and '41. The only prize that escaped him was the Indianapolis 500, in spite of four pole-position starts. This photo was taken at Oakland, California, in 1933, with Rex sitting in the Paul Fromm "Hisso" powered machine. A Hisso is half of a Hispano-Suiza V8 aircraft engine; one of the great legends of dirt track racing, Jud Larson got his start driving roadsters on the tough southwest Texas circuit in 1939. After WWII, Larson bounced around the southwest driving anything he could get his hands on, for any association that he could get a license with. His only championship came in 1948, when he took the A.A.A. Southwest midget title, but his barnstorming tactics made him a coast-to-coast celebrity. In 1956 he joined U.S.A.C. and caused an immediate sensation with his freewheeling driving style. Felled by a heat stroke in 1959, he returned in 1964 for two more seasons before a racing accident took his life. He is shown here with car owner John Pfrommer at Reading, Pennsylvania, in 1956 in the seat of Pfrommer's powder-blue-and-white Hillegas Offy sprinter. Check those knobby tires!

33

Left to right: Early racecars have charisma not usually exhibited in modern, faster, safer cars; the number 33 Kehoe car has a history, but we don't know much of it....

Vintage RACECARS

Photos by Dain Gingerelli

Elsewhere in Hop Up 2001, Jim Chini has shown an array of early roundy-round cars and their hot-rod-origin drivers. There are lots of these cars extant in various states of repair, disrepair and restoration reposing in museums, private collections and old sheds, and some are still exercised regularly in exhibitions and "demo" racing.

These collectible and historical artifacts do, then, have lives "after." Their community of devotees is small relative to motorsport stars like NASCAR, but the group enshrining the old flat-tails is more and more active in chronicling its history and mourning its losses. The losses are those suffered on-track throughout the century and from the rockin' chair in the century's last half.

Some heirs-apparent to the legendary cars and their history got together on a spring afternoon recently. At a one-mile thoroughbred track near the Hop Up Towers, Kenny Tucker brought the historically significant Holland Special for a joust with the Halmark Special. Also in attendance were Joe MacClelland and Tom Beggs in Joe's Cad-powered '35 Ford Roadster. It made for a true-to-the-day entourage as reflected in the accompanying photos.

From the top: Kenny Tucker "stands on it"; Halmark Special runs a dual-overhead-cam Hal head on Ford B block. It will be pushed off for demo runs in '01; Dain asked for victory portraits but produced no "Trophy Girl!"

The Holland Special was/is motivated by a Dodge flathead six, which made a unique and successful racing package. The car was driven by the likes of Andy Linden and other notable chauffeurs of its time; ultimately "Jiggler" Joe Gemsa owned it, turned it to Joe Mac, and Mac to Tucker. Its tow rig is a '50 Olds wagon from Tucker's extensive collection.

The other piece is the "Halmark Special," a D.O. Hal (Dual overhead-cam head on a B block—a poor man's Offy), Offy In and Out, Model A rear, '37 Ford tube axle and 'bones on a Clyde Adams chassis. Cad tow car is color-coordinated.

The third car didn't arrive in time for the photo shoot, so we caught up with it and its owner, Bob Kehoe, at the Antique Nationals picnic for a couple of snapshots. Bob is a 200 MPH Club Member (205.206 in a '53 Stude, 1970), so the sprinter is a logical addition to a well-rounded Hop Up Guy's garage. It was found through a lead at Mike Woodward's machine shop, resulting in the eventual purchase and loading-up of the car

From the top: Imagine them crossed-up, with plumes of dirt-obscuring the slower traffic, replete with appropriate noise!; Phill Whetstone lettered the Hal with typical flair; Holland Special features original early lettering from a long-gone sign painter.

From the top: Here's the sprinter on display at the Four Ever Four picnic preceding the Antique Nationals Drags; the four-port Riley on a B block was prepared by Bob Kehoe and his machine-shop buddies; the business office was extended 4 inches by Dennis Webb to allow the new owner to get in!

after decades of storage, complete with a bellypan full of water! Good thing we used aluminum, huh, Bob?!

It was running a Winfield flathead on the B block, but after a Taylor rebuild, the engine got a four-port Riley from the Bud Hand collection, and a new A transmission. The frame is pretty clearly a Clyde Adams example, noteworthy in and of itself, but any more specific history on the car is not available. Paint and lettering are original, so with some research, its heritage may be determined. Wheels are 16-inch drop-center Daytons, not period perfect but likely to have been added while the car was still being raced. Bob's a tall guy, so it took a 4-inch body stretch by Dennis Webb (moved tail back, left frame alone) to allow the new driver to enter for the hill climbs, drags and oval racing that the car is used for now. It is the only one of the three with this distinction.

The track had been recently graded for horse training but wasn't as compact or moist as it might have been for optimum dirt digging. The crews made the best of it, taking turns driving the Holland round and round, most of them getting a first-ever drive in an antique dirt car. It's about as thrilling and challenging as you might suspect (twitchy comes to mind), and all in attendance vowed to do it again as soon as all the cars are all running at the same time!

The track will be leveled for the construction of a truck terminal, eliminating a handy outlet for all this thermal energy. But that's okay; the HURT (Hop Up Racing Team) is resourceful and has other venues in mind, including the traditional Walt James Play Day at Willow Springs and other WRA and VARA sanctioned events!

Dain's photography tells you all you need to know about the day at the "mile," except the sound. Ya had ta be there!

T'N'A 'N' Chevrolet

Hop Up Guys continue to crave information on the Ts and As and Bs that founded our hobby. Some of us were born too late to have absorbed it by osmosis, so we offer this chapter in our civic-minded effort to inform, educate, and promote the screwing-up of restored old Fords.

ROAR with
GILMORE

GABBY GARRISON'S CHEVROLET SOUP JOB

Photos by Dain Gingerelli

Here we are in the T 'n' A section, and what has Hop Up wrought? A Chevrolet. A WHAT?!!! Yeah, fellers. Bowtie. Stovebolt. The one with all the wood.

Some people don't know that Chevrolet always outsold Ford once the T became aged and un-evolving. Kids at the time did the Hop Up deal to Chevys, too, and one of them was Gabby Garrison. His name may be familiar as the guy with the cool '25 T that Dain Gingerelli reported on in recent years (see attached picture) and found itself on the Hop Up web page generally getting the attention of anybody who is a student of "Teasing." The T was a copy of one of the soup jobs he did as a youth; this '26 Chevy Touring Car is another one.

It was during the depression, Gabby will remind you, and some of the more famous (read more affluent) kids were buying parts and hiring some things done. That doesn't sound too different than today, no? But Gabby, growing up in Long Beach, California, had to do most of it himself. Trading labor for parts, parts for parts, and rarely, a buck for parts, he did his '26 Chevrolet Touring with all the tricks of the day.

Gabby tells us that the already overhead-valve Chevrolet was discovered to breathe poorly because of its restrictive single exhaust port. Some clever rascal had noticed that the Oldsmobile (also an overhead four-barrel) had three exhaust ports and would bolt right up on the Chevy, even using a stock head gasket. Go figure that today, huh Podnuh? So he arranged to get one.

The next performance step was to note that there was no combustion chamber relief in the head at all. And since the pistons didn't run all the way up to the top of the deck, they'd mill the block a quarter-inch to enhance the squeeze! He did that, too. Somebody had ID'd Nash rock-

Above: Not all gow jobs were Fords, as Gabby Garrison will tell you. His Depression-era Chevy Touring Car has been reborn for the millennium with just a few concessions to modern technology. **Left to right**: Gabby is having a great time re-doing what he did back then. Is he the original Hop Up Guy?; the skull radiator cap was badass, even in the Thirties.

Gabby gained the right stance for his Chevy by mating an Essex axle with the original parallel front springs and massaging the rear leaves.

er arms as having a higher ratio, so they, Dodge valves, longer Durant rods, and a Burns intake with Studebaker Stromberg carb made the engine behave like a street prowler should.

The aesthetic formula was similar to the modern one: The car had to ride lower, so an Essex axle (right width, 3-inch net drop, virtually perfect bolt up to Chev parallel front springs), reversed spring eyes and leaf shenanigans in the rear took care of ride height. But what of that tall windscreen? Whack it. Install early Ford jointed stanchions, shorten them and discard the bottom glass, replace with hand-carved wooden panel painted black on the back and spruced up with aluminum sheet on the front. Whoa! Looks great up and also looks great folded forward for performance runs.

This shrinking of the profile causes the seat to be a little high, so you trim the seat riser 4 inches and...ah...poop! The gas tank is in there. Oh. You hang it out back under the spare, out of the way. And the spare? The stock angle (following the contour of the touring body and sloping downward toward the front of the car) is not jaunty. Get an old Ford spare mount, flip it and modify it so the spare is in the appropriate jaunty angle (like sports-type cars of the era, you see?), and then apply the Gilmore Red Lion spare tire cover that was a much-coveted accessory in the day. The interior was whatever you could afford or create your way into. And windwings. Yeah. Accessorisin.'

Next, we gotta do the modern wheel treatment. Easy. Use 19-inch wire wheels from a '31 Chevy, painted red. But we still got no mud flaps. What to do? Discarded oil field rubber belting material. Innovation, not invention!

The crowning glory, the final statement then, is the aftermarket skull radiator cap. We bad. We bad-long before we knew what bad was!

Gabby's millennium re-creation of his car is only subtly different than the above prescription for cool. Oversize stainless steel valves, homemade intake manifold with modern two-barrel carbie, and nice interior are the main differences. But this octogenarian is having a great time re-doing what he did with such pleasure back then. And one of the things that pleases him the most is that there are youngsters (graybeards?) who appreciate his iron—and him—in this time of apparently urgent evolution of fashion. Some things started out cool and stayed cool; Gabby is a special guy. A Hop Up Guy. Hell, he may be the original one.

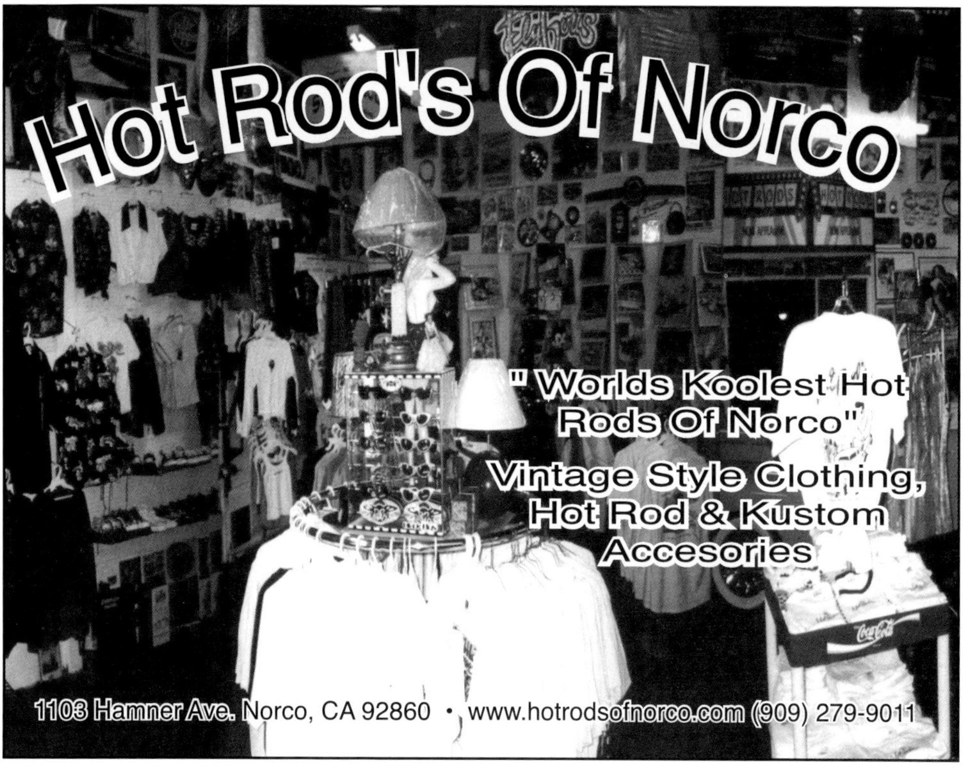
Hot Rod's Of Norco
" Worlds Koolest Hot Rods Of Norco"
Vintage Style Clothing, Hot Rod & Kustom Accesories
1103 Hamner Ave. Norco, CA 92860 • www.hotrodsofnorco.com (909) 279-9011

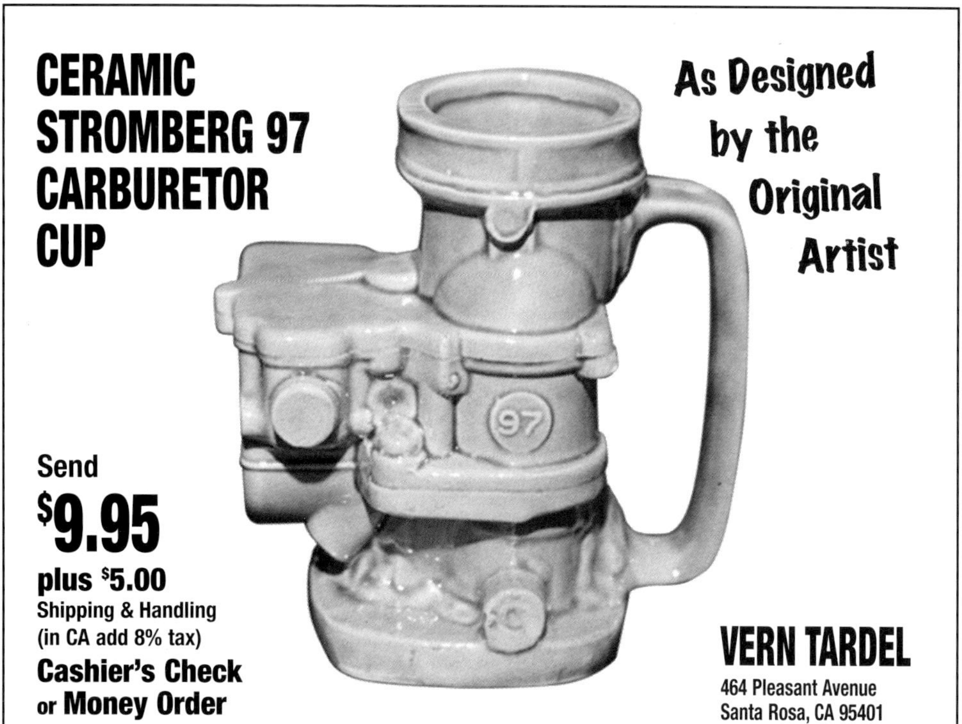
CERAMIC STROMBERG 97 CARBURETOR CUP
As Designed by the Original Artist
97
Send
$9.95
plus $5.00
Shipping & Handling
(in CA add 8% tax)
Cashier's Check or Money Order
VERN TARDEL
464 Pleasant Avenue
Santa Rosa, CA 95401

Poetry

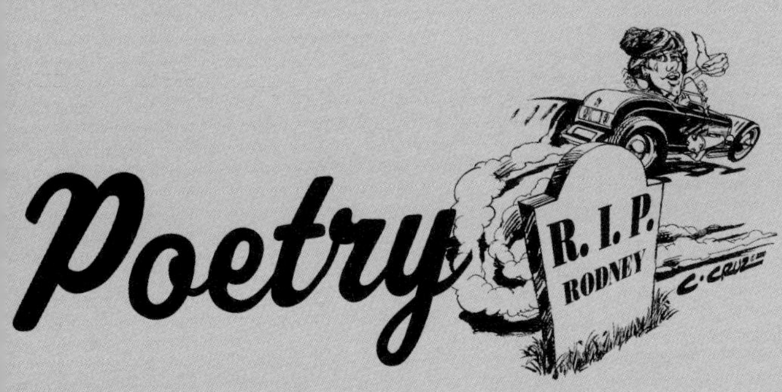

Hot Rod Poetry hasn't gotten as far as Cowboy Poetry into the consciousness of the unwashed. We, of course, don't care. It's not FOR the unwashed. It's for Hop Up Guys and Dolls. If you don't already get it, well, ya just ain't gonna get it.

Enjoy.

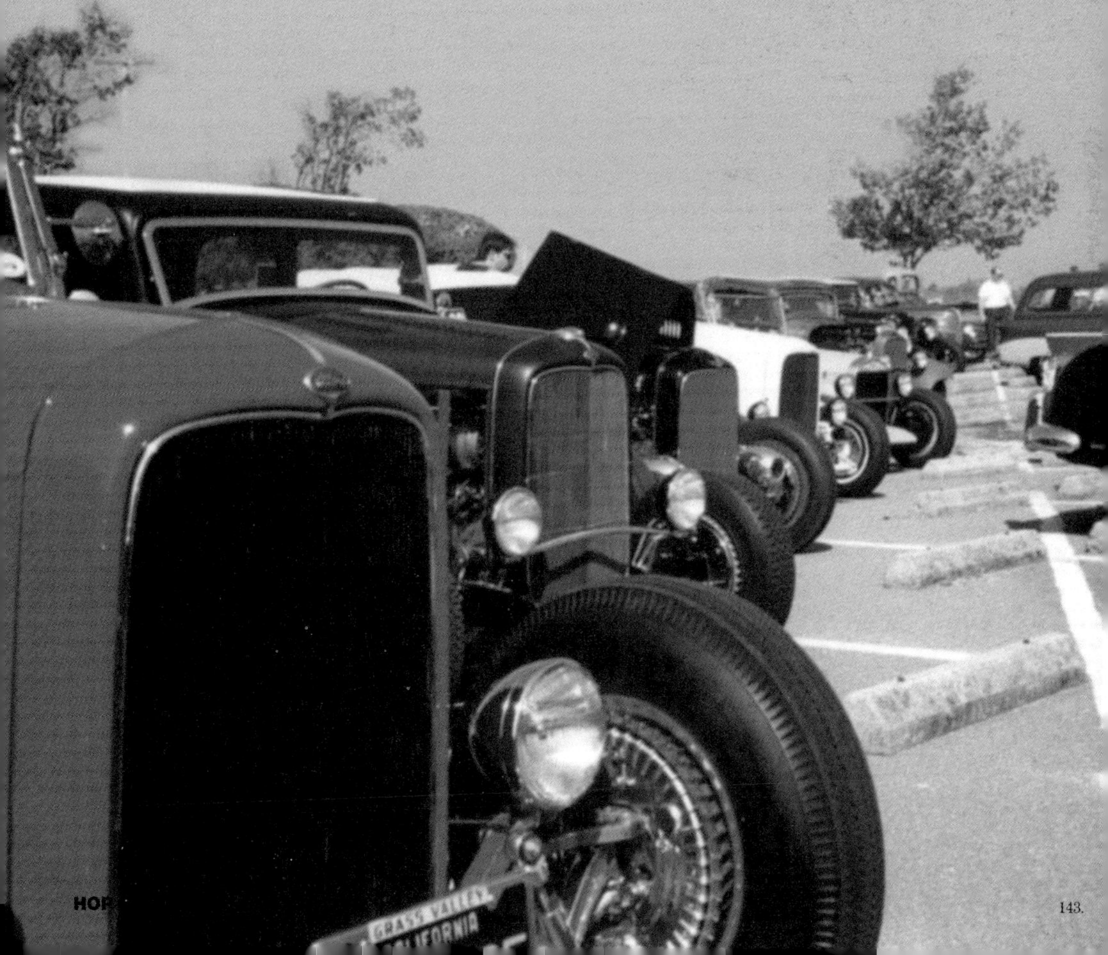

LAST WILL

You gotta admire the older guys
Whose rods have great patina,
With rubbed-through paint, and bias tires
And shades of Pasadena.

Plated parts with pits all green,
The fasteners rusted through,
Their character survived the years,
And that's the big "to do."

Every rodder has a dream
That one day he'll fulfill
When some old coot will die and leave
A roadster in his will.

The lucky guy is me, of course,
A most deserving soul,
Who'll love the car and wax it up
And make its drivetrain whole.

No guilt attached, the will was read,
And that you can't deny:
In spite of sons, and sons-in-law,
I'm just a bitchin guy.

How you gonna fault a dude
Who made a good impression?
Who knew the kind of trans they ran
And Winfield's "red" compression?

"This was what he wanted,"
Would say the grieving wife
"Go take the age-old roadster
And give it one more life."

But you all know, I needn't say,
It'd never frickin' happen.
Cuz if he died, all my good friends
Would have their jaws a-flappin'...

"That 'digger' shouldn't get the car,
Cuz he's got more than me,
And I know of a richer cat
(Who'll gladly pay MY fee.)"

So I'd be left with my own thoughts
To while away the time
And lookin' at my roadster
"I think it's past ITS prime."

It leaks a little fluid
From places front and back
With windshield pits and broken parts
Revealed up on the rack.

It burns some oil and makes a noise
When winding up in first
And according to the gas bill
It's developed quite a thirst.

The paint is shrunk and pitted
From gravel, rocks and bugs
The leather's cracked and faded
And there's heel-holes in the rug.

Maybe I've already got it—
The old rod of my dreams?
In my own garage for all these years
At least that's how it seems!

We've been so close I'd never seen
The fading setting in.
But we have aged together
Bad paint, its "wrinkled" skin.

So I don't need the other car
To satisfy my need
Mine will go just as far
To sate "patina greed."

And then it will be MY turn
To make the final plan;
Determine who deserves it;
Select the lucky man.

So if my ol' heart seizes
And someday it just might;
I've told my wife to crush the car
And save you guys the fight!

—Mort 2000